TH

POC

C000171020

1995/1996

Editor - Charles Heyman

Copyright c R & F (Military Publishing) 1995

ISBN 0 85052 458X

First Edition 1984
Second Edition 1987
Third Edition 1991
Fourth Edition 1993
Fifth Edition 1995

Price £4.95 (Mail Order £5.25)

There are special rates for purchases of more than 10 books.

From : Pen & Sword Books Ltd
47 Church Street
Barnsley S70 2AS

Telephone : 01226-734222   Fax : 01226-734438

The information in this publication has been gathered from unclassified sources.

Front & Rear Cover: Royal Artillery Air Defence Units with Javelin
Surface to Air Missiles.
(Photographs by Permission of P-Info HQ 5 Div)

THE BRITISH ARMY
A POCKET GUIDE

This, fifth edition of the British Army Guide appears at a time when there is continuing debate about the future role of the British Army, especially following recent events in Northern Ireland. This is not unusual and there appears to have been an ongoing debate about the future of the British Army that started during Cromwell's time, and has continued ever since.

We have the good fortune to live in a relatively safe and stable society and it is very easy to forget, as Rudyard Kipling wrote, that safety and stability is very dependent on "uniforms that guard you while you sleep". To a great extent defence depends on money, and a nation generally gets the defence that it pays for.

The politicians have a difficult equation to square. Running defence forces down to an unacceptable level invites internal instability and possible external aggression. However, spending more on defence than is absolutely necessary during a time of peace can be equally damaging. Neighbouring countries become fearful, and their parallel rise in defence spending creates an arms race that can spiral out of control. Internal economic deprivation as a result of high defence spending creates tensions that can result in political collapse of the type that we have seen recently in Eastern Europe. There is a difficult balance that the politicians need to achieve and they are not to be envied in their task. Currently, we believe that this balance is about right, but is would be extremely easy to tip the scales in the wrong direction.

We will make two confident predictions knowing that we will not be proved wrong. The first is that during the next ten years countries without credible defences will be threatened by countries with large and aggressive military forces. At worst, nations that overlook the importance of their defences will be overrun, and their populations enslaved. At best their behaviour will be modified and their freedom of action limited. The second prediction is that the threat, when it appears will come from the most unexpected direction. "Ready for Anything" would be a good motto for the British Army in the years ahead - remembering that the defence of the United Kingdom is the first and highest priority.

"There is a great unwillingness amongst men to face the cruel facts of history and to accept harrowing experiences of the past as sure evidence of more to come".

John Alden - The History of Human Society

CONTENTS

(CHAPTER 1 - USEFUL INFORMATION)

(UK Statistics)

Population - 56,696,600

Population Strengths for Military Analysis:

Age Group:	13-17	18-22	23-32
Men	1,833,500	2,041,800	4,430,600
Women	1,744,300	1,942,300	4,253,900

Government:

The executive government is vested nominally in the Crown, but for practical purposes in a committee of Ministers that is known as the Cabinet. The head of the ministry and leader of the Cabinet is the Prime Minister. For the implementation of policy the Cabinet is dependent upon the support of a majority of the Members of Parliament in the House of Commons. Within the Cabinet defence matters are the responsibility of the Secretary of State for Defence.

Total British Armed Forces (as at 1 April 1995)

Regular: 241,000; Locally Entered 7,200; Regular Reserves 259,600; Volunteer Reserves 71,100; Cadet Forces 135,800; MOD Civilians 142,300.

Army 120,000; Royal Navy 51,000; Royal Air Force 70,000; (Note: Royal Navy figure includes some 7,300 Royal Marines.)

Strategic Forces: 3 x Resolution Class submarines each with 16 x Polaris A-3TK Submarine Launched Ballistic Missiles (SLBM). 1 x Vanguard Class submarine with 16 x Trident D5 SLBM - probably becoming operational in 1995.

Navy: 51,000: 12 x Submarines; 3 x Aircraft Carriers; 35 x Destroyers and Frigates; 18 x Mine Counter Measures Vessels; 33 x Patrol Craft; 3 x Harrier Squadrons; 13 x Helicopter Squadrons; 3 x Commando Groups: Royal Fleet Auxiliary - 2 x Large Fleet Tankers; 3 x Small Fleet Tankers; 3 x Support Tankers; 5 x Fleet Replenishment Ships; 1 x Helicopter Support Ship; 5 x Landing Ships; 1 x Forward Repair Ship.

Merchant Naval Vessels Registered in the UK: 384 x Offshore Support & Fishing Vessels; 34 x Tankers; 91 x General Cargo Vessels; 3 x Cruise Ships; 46 x Roll on - Roll off Ferries; 58 x Tugs. (Note: There are 47 x Tankers and 14 x General Cargo Vessels registered in overseas Crown Territories).

Air Force: 70,000; 6 x Strike/Attack Squadrons; 5 x Offensive Support Squadrons; 6 x Air Defence Squadrons; 3 x Maritime Patrol Squadrons; 5 x Reconnaissance Squadrons; 1 x Airborne Early Warning Squadron; 13 x Transport Squadrons; 3 x Tanker Squadrons; 2 x Search and Rescue Squadrons; 5 x Surface to Air Missile Squadrons; 4 x Ground Defence Squadrons.

Army: 120,000 (including some 5,000 Gurkhas); 1 x Corps Headquarters in Germany (ARRC); 1 x Armoured Divisional HQ in Germany; 1 x Divisional HQ in UK; 3 x Brigade Headquarters in Germany; 17 x Brigade Headquarters in UK; 1 x Airborne Brigade in UK.

British Army Major Units

(at 1 Jan 1995)	Germany	UK	Elsewhere	TA
Armoured Regts	6	3	-	-
Armoured Recce Regts	2	1	-	5
Infantry Battalions	6	33	2	36 (1)
Gurkha Battalions	-	1	3	-
SAS Regiments	-	1	-	2
Army Air Corps Regiments	1	4	-	-
Artillery Field Regts	3	6	-	2
Heavy Regts MLRS	2	1	-	-
Air Defence Regts	2	2	-	3
HAC	-	-	-	1
Engineer Regiments	5	6	1 (2)	9
Signals Regiments	4	7	2	11
EW Regiment	1	-	-	-
Equipment Support Bns	4	1	-	4
Logistic Regiments	9	15	1	11
Fd Ambulances/Hospitals	4	9	-	23

Note (1) Excludes the 6 x Home Service Battalions of the Royal Irish Regiment. (2) The Queen's Gurkha Engineers;

British Army Equipment Summary

Armour: 372 x Challenger 1; 386 Challenger 2 on order; 140 x Sabre (approx); 88 x Striker; 290 x Scimitar; 2,000 x Fv 432; 789 x MCV 80 Warrior; 400 x Spartan; 644 x Saxon.

Awaiting Disposal - Approx 850 x Chieftain; 271 x Scorpion.

Artillery: 500 x 81mm Mortar; 2093 x 51mm Light Mortar; 50 x M109A1; 179 x AS 90 on order; 62 x 227mm MLRS (deliveries continue); 72 x FH 70; 212 x 105mm Light Gun.

Air Defence: 120 x Rapier Fire Units; 40 x Tracked Rapier; 382 x Javelin Launchers; 135 x Starstreak HVM deliveries commencing.

Army Aviation: 126 x Lynx ; 30 x Scout; 159 Gazelle; 7 x BN-2; 7 x DHC2 and 21 Chipmunk (for training). Helicopters available from RAF- 32 x Chinook; 54 x Wessex; 37 x Puma.

The Defence Budget

> "You need three things to win a war,
> Money, money and more money".

Trivulzio (1441-1518)

The UK Government plans to spend the following amounts on defence during the next three years:-

> 1994-95 - £22.77 billion.
> 1995-96 - £21.72 billion.
> 1996-97 - £22.23 billion.

Overall Defence Expenditure is expected to fall by about 14% in real terms between 1992-93 and 1996-97, with defence spending representing approximately 3.8% of GDP (Gross Domestic Product) in 1992-93 and declining to about 2.9% of GDP in 1996-97. In 1985 Defence expenditure represented 5.2% of GDP.

An excellent illustration of the changes in UK Defence Expenditure are a comparison of defence spending totals that have been rounded/adjusted to 1993-94 prices:

> 1970-71 - £16.46 billion
> 1975-76 - £22.19 billion
> 1980-81 - £23.79 billion
> 1985-86 - £27.84 billion
> 1990-91 - £25.45 billion
> 1995-96 - £21.72 billion (planned)

The total Central Government Expenditure plans for the FY 1995-96 are budgeted at £305 billion and for comparison purposes the Government's major expenditure programmes during FY 1995-96 are as follows:

Defence	£21.72 billion
Overseas Aid	£2.36 billion
Health	£32.96 billion
Transport	£4.39 billion
Housing	£6.90 billion
Home Office	£6.41 billion
Education	£10.96 billion
Social Security	£87.07 billion
Agriculture	£3.02 billion
Employment	£3.46 billion
Legal Departments	£2.80 billion
Local Government	£30.29 billion
Scotland	£14.11 billion
Wales	£6.63 billion
Northern Ireland	£7.30 billion
Debt Interest	£24.50 billion
Miscellaneous	£40.12 billion

The breakdown of the 1994-95 Defence Budget figure of £22.77 billion pounds can be shown in percentage terms for all three services as follows:

Equipment Purchases -	37.7%
Service Personnel -	29.0% (pay & allowances)
Civilian Personnel -	12.4%
Works Buildings & Land -	8.0%
Miscellaneous Stores etc -	12.9%

The equipment expenditure figure can be broken down further, to reveal that during the 1994-95 Financial Year a total of £5.8 billion pounds will be spent, with money going to the services as follows:

Sea Systems -	£2.515 billion
Land Systems -	£1.876 billion
Air Systems -	£3.033 billion
General Support -	£1.362 billion
Research -	£0.604 billion
Total -	£9.390 billion

Note: In general Sea, Land and Air Systems relate to Naval, Army and Air Force expenditure.

Some of the more interesting Army equipment expenditure figures for the 1992-93 Financial Year (the latest year for which the figures are available) are amongst the following:

Guns, Small Arms and NBC Defence Stores -	£137 million
Ammunition, Mines and Explosives -	£289 million
Armoured Fighting Vehicles -	£200 million
Load Carrying Vehicles -	£226 million
Engineering Equipment -	£25 million
Guided Weapons -	£243 million
Communications -	£108 million
Surveillance Equipment -	£64 million
Maintenance -	£374 million

Army Expenditure (Top Level Budget Holders - TLB)

During 1994-95 Army expenditure figures are amongst the following:

UK Land Forces

Scotland -	£96.4 million
Eastern District -	£393.8 million
London District -	£161.1 million
Southern District -	£590.9 million
Wales & Western District -	£160.4 million
Army Doctrine & Training -	£471.6 million
Administration -	£136.9 million
Reserves & Cadets -	£82.3 million
GOC Northern Ireland -	£542.3 million
	(£2,635.7) million

UK Support Command (Germany)

1 UK Armoured Division -	£710.5 million
Personnel, Training & Community Support Services -	£292.0 million
Works projects, Logistics & Equipment Support Services -	£231.4 million
	(£1,233.8 million)

Overseas Garrisons

Belize -	£14.9 million*
Falkland Islands -	£67.8 million
Gibraltar -	£57.6 million
Hong Kong -	£20.4 million
Cyprus -	£205.2 million
SBA Administration (Cyprus) -	£9.3 million
Operations & Security -	£22.6 million
Overseas Operations -	£2.3 million
TLB Sponsored Units -	£41.8 million
	£423.7 million

Note: The vast majority of the Belize garrison was withdrawn at the end of 1994 and a small training team left in place.

Army Personnel - Adjutant General (TLB)

Manning & Recruitment -	£76.9 million
Army Trainees -	£135.1 million
Personnel Support -	£38.2 million
Army Personnel Administration & Services -	£76.6 million
	£578.9 million

Army Logistics - Quartermaster General (TLB)

Equipment Support -	£515.5 million
Logistic Support -	£376.0 million
Logistic Policy & Services -	£54.1 million
Communications & Information Systems -	£36.7 million
	(£963.9 million)

The high unit costs of individual items of equipment illustrate the problems faced by defence planners when working out their annual budgets. At 1994 prices the following items cost:

Kinetic Energy Round for Challenger	£1,500 each
Individual Weapon (IW)	£570 each
5.56mm round for IW .90p One Rapier Missile	£35,000
One Challenger Tank	£2 million (approx)
Tornado Air Defence Fighter	£20 million
PRC 351 VHF Radio	£6,000 each
Combat High Boot	£40 per pair
Harrier GR5	£14.2 million
Lynx Helicopter	£6.25 million
Starstreak Missile	£100,000 each
Trigat (MR) Missile	£25,000 each (estimate).
Attack Helicopter	£17 million (region)

During 1992-93 the British Army spent £106.2 million on fuel for heating and lighting. During 1993-94 the MOD's telephone bill was £61.4 million.

Defence Budgets - NATO Comparison

For ease of conversions from national currencies amounts are shown in US$. The nations of the North Atlantic Treaty Organisation (NATO), of which the United Kingdom is a member state, spent some US$418.5 billion on defence during 1994.

NATO Defence Budget Analysis

NATO Defence Expenditure 1994 -   US$418.5 billion
NATO Defence Expenditure 1994 (less USA) -   US$156.8 billion
NATO (European Nations) Defence Expenditure 1994 US$145.2 billion
-

The next table shows the defence budget for each NATO nation during 1994.

USA	US$ 261.7 billion
France	US$ 35.6 billion
UK	US$ 34.0 billion
Germany	US$ 28.6 billion
Italy	US$ 16.1 billion
Canada	US$ 11.6 billion
Netherlands	US$ 7.2 billion
Spain	US$ 5.8 billion
Turkey	US$ 4.6 billion
Greece	US$ 3.3 billion
Norway	US$ 3.2 billion
Belgium	US$ 2.6 billion
Denmark	US$ 2.6 billion
Portugal	US$ 1.5 billion
Luxembourg	US$ 106 million

Note: Iceland has no military expenditure although it remains a member of NATO.

An interesting comparison is made by the total national defence budget divided by the total number of full time personnel in all three services. Figures for the top five world defence spending nations are as follows:-

Ranking	Nation	1994 Defence Budget	Total Service Personnel	Cost Per Serviceman
1	USA	US$261.7 bn	1,650,500	US$158,558
2	Japan	US$42.1 bn	237,700	US$177,114
3	France	US$35.6 bn	409,600	US$86,914
4	UK	US$34.0 bn	254,300	US$133,700
5	Germany	US$28.6 bn	367,300	US$77,865

Note: Russia should probably be the second nation in this table, but because of the effects of inflation it is currently impossible to make a meaningful conversion from Roubles to US$. Problems in October 1994 when the Rouble fell from around 1,800 to 3,000 to the US Dollar have made the problem worse. Most defence analysts are using a figure of US$30 billion as the Russian 1994 defence budget.

British Army Statistics:

Strength of The Regular Army (1 January 1995)

Armour	12 Regiments (1)
Royal Artillery	16 Regiments (2)
Royal Engineers	12 Regiments (3)
Infantry	41 Battalions (4)
Special Air Service	1 Regiment
Army Air Corps	6 Regiments
Signals	14 Regiments (5)
Equipment Support	5 Battalions
Logistics	25 Regiments (6)
Medical	13 Hospitals/Field Ambulances

Notes: (1) Includes 1 x Training Regiment. (2) Includes 1 x Training Regiment. (3) Includes the Queen's Gurkha Engineers. (4) Excludes the 6 x Battalions that comprise the Home Service Element of the Royal Irish Regiment. (5) Includes 2 x Training Regiments. (6) Includes 3 x Combat Service Support Battalions that have a mix of REME, RAMC and RLC personnel). In general these Battalions/Regiments are commanded by Lt Colonels and have a strength of between 500 and 800 personnel.

Strength of the Territorial Army (1 January 1995)

Armour	5 Regiments
Royal Artillery	6 Regiments (1)
Royal Engineers	9 Regiments
Infantry	36 Battalions
Special Air Service	2 Regiments
Signals	11 Regiments
Equipment Support	4 Battalions
Logistics	11 Regiments
Medical	23 Hospitals/Field Ambulances
Special Air Service	2 Regiments

Notes: (1) Includes Honourable Artillery Company (HAC).

Deployment of The Regular Army (As at 1 April 1994)

	Officers	Soldiers
UK Land Forces		
Army Doctrine & Training	2,100	9,400
Eastern District	900	10,800
Scotland	200	1,900

London District	400	4,900
Southern District	1,400	16,100
Wales & Western District	300	2,500
Administration	800	1,600
	6,100	**47,200**

UK Support Command (Germany)

1st (UK) Armoured Division	1,700	24,400
Personnel & Community Support	800	4,500
Logistics & Equipment Support	100	700
	2,600	**29,600**

GOC Northern Ireland	**800**	**10,600**

Overseas Garrisons - Including RAF and RN

Falkland Island	100	1,600
Gibraltar	100	700
Hong Kong	400	1,600
Cyprus	400	4,100
SBA Security (Cyprus)	200	200
Overseas Operations	200	100
Other	100	100
	(1,600)	(8,400)

Note: The above figures relate to tri-service garrisons. Army figures for various areas are as follows:

Gibraltar	147
Cyprus	2,817
Near East & Gulf	202
Hong Kong	1,441
Former Yugoslavia	3,500 (detached from UK and Germany)
Brunei	850
Far East Elsewhere	194

Adjutant General (TLB)

Manning & Recruitment	200	700
Army Trainees	1,800	8,100
Personnel Support	-	100
Personnel Administration	200	600
	2,200	**9,500**

Quartermaster General (TLB)

Equipment Support	200	600
Logistic Support	300	2,000
Logistic Policy & Services	100	300

Comms & Information Systems	100	200
	700	**3,100**

(Manning Figures (Including personnel under training)

Regular Army (As at 1 April 1994)

	1994	1990
Trained Officers	14,000	16,200
Trained Soldiers	102,100	121,000
Untrained Officers	900	1,200
Untrained Soldiers	6,000	14,400
	123,000	**152,800**

Note: 1990 Figures are given for comparison purposes.

Regular Army Reserves (As at 1 April 1994)

	1994	1980
Regular Reserves	192,500	133,100
Territorial Army	65,000*	63,300

*Includes Royal Irish Regiment - Home Service Element

Recruitment - Regular Army (During Financial Year 1993/94)

	(1993-94)	(1990/91)	(1980/81)
Officers	752	1,454	1,489
Soldiers	8,824	16,048	27,382
Total	**9,576**	**17,502**	**28,871**

Note: Previous years figures are given for comparison.

Outflow - Regular Army (During Financial Year 1993/94)

	(1993-94)	(1990/91)	(1980/81)
Officers	2,270	1,860	1,497
Soldiers	18,651	20,964	20,422
Total	**20,921**	**22,824**	**21,919**

Army Uniformed Medical Personnel (At 1 Apr 1993)

Doctors	522
Dentists	178
Nurses	4,288 (Figure includes males, females and nursing support staff).

Note: 1993 Figures are the latest available.

Army Cadet Force

	(1 Apr 1994)	(1 Apr 1980)
Total Cadets	63,900	74,600

100 Years Ago - Strength of the British Army (As at 1 May 1895)

Household Cavalry	1,316	(800)
Cavalry of the Line	18,388	(6,000)
Horse Artillery	3,781	
Field Artillery	14,308	(14,000 Artillery
Mountain Artillery	1,293	total)
Garrison Artillery	17,312	
Royal Engineers	7,424	(10,000)
Foot Guards	6,032	(4,000)
Infantry of the Line	135,175	(29,000)
Colonial Corps	5,070	
Army Service Corps	3,523	(20,000 RLC)
Ordnance Staff	857	
Armourers	318	(12,000 REME)
Medical Services	2,482	(4,000)
	217,279	(120,000)

Note: To allow a comparison to be made, the figures in brackets are our estimates of the approximate 1995 totals.

Animals on Strength (As at 1 Oct 1994)

Horses	486
Dogs	1700
Goats	2 (Regimental Mascots)
Black Buck	1 (Regimental Mascot)
Ram	1 (Regimental Mascot)
Shetland Pony	2 (Regimental Mascots)
Wolf Hound	1 (Regimental Mascot)
Drum Horse	1 (Regimental Mascot)

CHAPTER 2 - ORGANISATIONS

"The ideal General Staff should in peacetime do nothing! They deal in an intangible stuff called thought. Their main business consists of thinking out what the enemy may do and what their Commanding Generals ought to do, and the less they clank their spurs the better".

General Sir Ian Hamilton (1853-1947)

Until 1963 the British Army was an organisation almost entirely independent from the other two fighting services. The Army had its own headquarters at The War Office in London, and the subsequent duplication of effort, especially at headquarters level combined with the lack of a central planning staff resulted in a serious loss of efficiency.

In 1963 the three independent service ministries were merged to form the present Ministry of Defence (MOD). This massive organisation which directly affects the lives of about half a million servicemen, reservists and MOD employed civilians is controlled by The Secretary of State for Defence who chairs The Defence Council. This Defence Council is the organisation that makes the policy decisions, to ensure that the three services are run efficiently, and in accordance with the wishes of the government of the day. The composition of The Defence Council is as follows:

Defence Council

The Secretary of State for Defence
Minister of State (Armed Forces)
Minister of State (Defence Procurement)
Parliamentary Under-Secretary of State for the Armed Forces
Chief Scientific Adviser
Chief of Defence Procurement
Chief of Personnel & Logistics
Chief of the Defence Staff
Vice-Chief of the Defence Staff
Chief of the Naval Staff and First Sea Lord
Chief of the Air Staff
Chief of the General Staff
Second Permanent Under Secretary of State

The routine management of the Army is the responsibility of The Army Board. The composition of The Army Board is shown in the next diagram.

The Army Board
The Secretary of State for Defence
Minister of State (Armed Forces)

Minister of State (Defence Procurement)
Parliamentary Under-Secretary of State for the Armed Forces
Chief of the General Staff
Second Permanent Under Secretary of State
Adjutant General
Quartermaster General
Master General of the Ordnance
Commander in Chief (Land Command)
Commander UK Support Command (Germany)
Assistant Chief of the General Staff

Decisions made by The Defence Council or the Army Board are acted upon by the military staff at the various headquarters world-wide. The Chief of the General Staff is the officer responsible for the Army's contribution to the national defence effort and he maintains control through the commander and the staff branches of each of these headquarters. Each military headquarters is organised along exactly the same lines with identical branches at each level in the chain of command.

Staff Branches

The Staff Branches that you would expect to find at every military headquarters from the Ministry of Defence (MOD) down to Brigade level are as follows:

Commander - Usually a general who commands the formation.

Chief of Staff - The officer who runs the headquarters on a day-to-day basis and who often acts as a second-in-command.

G1 Branch - Responsible for personnel matters including manning, discipline and personal services.

G2 Branch - Responsible for intelligence and security

G3 Branch - Responsible for operations including staff duties, exercise planning, training, operational requirements, combat development & tactical doctrine.

G4 Branch - Logistics and quartering.

G5 Branch - Civil and military co-operation

Chain of Command

The Army is controlled from the MOD via three subsidiary headquarters and a number of smaller headquarters world-wide. The Joint Headquarters (JHQ) at Northwood in Middlesex is currently being established (early 1995). This headquarters is in place to ensure that the three services are better placed to adapt to a developing crisis, without dislocation, upheaval or sending the political signals that the activation of an ad hoc Joint Headquarters generally causes. The following diagram illustrates this chain-of-command as from 1 April 1995.

Chain of Command

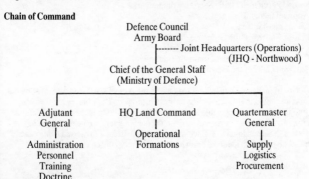

HQ Land Command

Following the MOD's "Front Line First" study plans were drawn up to reorganise HQ United Kingdom Land Forces (HQ UKLF) in a new formation designated HQ Land Command. Operational from 1 April 1995 HQ Land Command will be located at Erskine Barracks, Wilton near Salisbury and will control 72% of the troops in the British Isles and almost 100% of its fighting capability. The first Commander-in-Chief Land Command will be the present Commander-in-Chief United Kingdom Land Forces, General Sir John Wilsey.

Land Commands's role will be to deliver and sustain the Army's operational capability, whenever required throughout the world, and the Command will comprise all operational troops in Great Britain, Germany, Nepal and Brunei, together with the Army Training Teams in Canada, Belize and Kenya.
Land Command will comprise nearly 72,000 trained Army personnel - 72% of the Army's total, and will be the largest single Top Level Budget in Defence, with a budget of just under £3 Billion. It will contain all the Army's fighting equipment, including attack helicopters, Challenger 2 tanks, Warrior Infantry Fighting Vehicles, AS90 (the new artillery gun) and the Multi-Launched Rocket System (MLRS).

Land Command will be one of the three central commands in the British Army, the other two being the Adjutant General (with responsibility for administration, personnel and training) and the Quartermaster General (responsible for supply and logistics). The Command will be responsible for providing all the Army's fighting troops throughout the World. These are organised into eight formations and will be commanded by Major Generals.

The Structure of Land Command

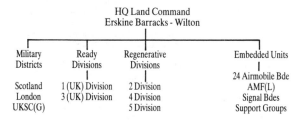

HQ Land Command
Erskine Barracks - Wilton

Military Districts	Ready Divisions	Regenerative Divisions	Embedded Units
			24 Airmobile Bde
Scotland	1 (UK) Division	2 Division	AMF(L)
London	3 (UK) Division	4 Division	Signal Bdes
UKSC(G)		5 Division	Support Groups

Overseas Detachments

Note: Overseas Detachments include Belize, Canada, Brunei and Nepal and Kenya. Garrisons in Northern Ireland, Cyprus and the Falkland Islands are commanded from the MOD via JHQ.

Ready Divisions

Two "Ready" Divisions: the 1st (UK) Armoured Division, based in Germany, and the 3rd (UK) Division in the United Kingdom. Both of these divisions are earmarked to form part of the Allied Command Europe Rapid Reaction Corps (ARRC), NATO's premier strategic formation; but they also have the flexibility to be employed on rapid reaction tasks or in support of other Defence Roles. In addition to their operational roles, they also command the Army units in specified geographic areas: in the case of the 1st Division, this area is made up of the garrisons in Germany where the Division's units are based; and in the case of the 3rd Division the South West of England.(Regenerative Divisions)

Regenerative Divisions

Three Regenerative Divisions, based on old Districts in the United Kingdom. These are the 2nd Division (replacing Eastern District) with its Headquarters at York, the 4th Division with its Headquarters at Aldershot, and the 5th Division (replacing the old Wales and Western District) with its Headquarters at Shrewsbury. These Regenerative divisions are responsible for all Army units within their boundaries, and could provide the core for three new divisions, should the Army be required to expand to meet a major international threat.

Districts

Three Districts will remain: Scotland, London, and the United Kingdom Support Command (Germany). Scotland and London are responsible for all Army units within their boundaries; the United Kingdom Support Command (Germany) with its Headquarters at Rheindahlen has similar responsibilities, but also provides essential support functions for the 1st Division and the Headquarters of the ARRC.

These eight divisions or district areas are further sub-divided into brigades and garrisons, which also have a varying mix of operational and infrastructure support responsibilities. As a result of the Defence Costs Studies, some brigade headquarters, which previously had purely operational functions, have been amalgamated with garrison headquarters to achieve savings and greater efficiency.

Embedded into this structure are all the other force elements which represent Land Command's operational capability. They include:

24 Airmobile Brigade, based in Colchester which is part of the Multi-National Division (Centre), an airmobile division with its headquarters in Rheindahlen.

The United Kingdom element of the ACE Mobile Force (Land), with its Headquarters and logistic elements at Bulford and an infantry battalion at Dover.

Three Signal Brigades (one of which is in Germany).

Two Combat Service Support Groups (one of which is in Germany).

Various additional units which are earmarked for the ACE Rapid Reaction Corps or for National Defence tasks.

The overseas detachments in Canada, Belize, Brunei and Nepal are commanded directly from Headquarters Land Command at Wilton. The Review of the Army Command Structure recommended that the Army should be organised into three central commands and that doctrine and training should be the responsibility of the Adjutant General rather than the Command-in-Chief. Therefore Headquarters Doctrine and Training at Upavon, Wiltshire, does not form part of Land Command (although it was part of United Kingdom Land Forces until 1993).

Defence Roles and Responsibilities

Land Command's role is to deliver and sustain the Army's operational capability wherever and whenever it is required. The Army's roles are based on the three major National Defence Roles, which remain as follows:

Defence Role 1 - To ensure the protection and security of the United Kingdom and its dependent territories, even when there is no immediate external threat.

Defence Role 2 - To ensure against any major external threat to the United Kingdom and its allies.

Defence Role 3 - To contribute to promoting the United Kingdom's wider security interests through the maintenance of international peace and stability.

Land Command's responsibilities will include the following:

Although Land Command will not be responsible for running operations in Northern Ireland, Cyprus and the Falkland Islands, it will provide the operational troops for them. Some 12,000 troops are involved in Northern Ireland at present, either deployed in the Province or training for deployment; and a further 5000 are deployed to Cyprus and the Falklands.

National operations and operations in support of the United Nations. The most significant UN operation at present are the 4,000 Army troops in Bosnia; but other troops are also deployed in Azerbaijan and Georgia at the present.

Some 500 troops are involved at any one time in MoD-sponsored equipment trials, demonstrations and exhibitions.

Public Duties take up two/three battalions at any one time.

All troops not otherwise operationally committed are also available to provide Military Aid to the Civil Authorities in the United Kingdom.

Headquarters Land Command will assume a number of new responsibilities, some of which have been delegated from MoD as part of recent reviews. These include: The Commitments Plot - Control of the Operational Tour Plot, the Arms Plot (the rotation of Armoured, Artillery and Infantry units between stations), the Formation Training Plot, and the provision of assistance to trials and studies.

Collective Training - Including responsibility for armoured battlegroup training at the British Army Training Unit at Suffield in Canada.

Land Command Divisional/District Summaries

1 (UK) Armd Div - The 1st Armoured Division was formed in 1940 adopting the charging rhino (the most heavily "armoured" animal) as its insignia in 1942 prior to El Alamein. Since the Second World War the Division has been retitled three times and became the 1st (United Kingdom) Armoured Division in 1993, having successfully fought in the Gulf War of 1991. The Division has its headquarters at Herford in Germany and commands three Armoured Brigades situated throughout North West Germany.

2 Div - The 2nd Division has responsibility for the whole of Eastern England excluding Essex. Though the Division was first formed in 1809 to fight in the Peninsular War, the crossed keys sign was not adopted until 1940 when it was reconstituted in England after Dunkirk. Its most famous engagement was during

the Burma Campaign in 1944 when, at the battle for Kohima, the tide against the Japanese Army finally turned. The Divisional Headquarters is in York.

3 (UK) Div - The 3rd (United Kingdom) Division is the only operational (Ready) Division in the UK. The Division has a mix of capabilities encompassing armoured, airborne and wheeled elements in its two mechanised brigades and one airborne brigade. The Division which was first formed during the Napoleonic Wars now also has responsibility for South-West England. The "Iron-Triangle" insignia was chosen for it in the early part of World War II by its commander then, Major General B L Montgomery. The Divisional Headquarters is in Bulford.

4 Div - The 4th Division has military responsibility for South East England, including Bedfordshire, Essex and Hertfordshire and its headquarters is in Aldershot. It was previously based in Germany until 1992 as an armoured division. The division now has three brigades under command, 2 Brigade based in Dover, 24 Brigade in Colchester and 145 Brigade in Aldershot. The divisional symbol is the Tiger.

5 Div - The 5th Division has responsibility for military units and establishments in Wales, the West Midlands and the North West of England and the Headquarters is in Shrewsbury. The Division emblem, inherited from Wales and Western District, depicts the Welsh Dragon, the cross of St Chad (7th Century Bishop of Mercia), and the Red Rose of Lancaster. The Fifth Division fought at Waterloo and played a significant part in the endeavours of the BEF in both World Wars.

UKSC(G) - The United Kingdom support Command (Germany) has responsibility for British Army Troops on the Continent of Europe that are not part of 1st (United Kingdom) Armoured Division. Its headquarters replaces that of the British Army of the Rhine, whose sign it has adopted. The new headquarters is located at Rheindahlen.

SCOTLAND - The Army in Scotland is commanded from a Headquarters at Craigiehall, Edinburgh which has responsibility for the entire national territory of Scotland including the Western and Northern Islands. The distinguishing flag of Army Headquarters Scotland is a Lion Rampant superimposed on a red, black and red background.

LONDIST - Headquarters London District was formed in 1906. It has responsibility for units that are located within the Greater London Area as well as in Windsor. The activity for which the Headquarters and the District is most well known is State Ceremonial and Public Duties in the Capital. The district insignia shows the Sword of St Paul representing the City of London and the Mural Crown representing the County of London. The District has its Headquarters in Horse Guards.

18

3 (UK) Division

Following plans for the reorganisation of NATO Forces on the Central Front during 1992, the HQ of the 3rd (UK) Armoured Division moved from its old location at Soest in Germany to Bulford in Wiltshire, where it became 3(UK) Division part of the NATO ARRC (Allied Rapid Reaction Corps). In the event of hostilities it will move to the ARRC area of operations on the European mainland or worldwide as necessary. During operations 3 (UK) Div equipment totals (excluding 3 Cdo Bde) could resemble the following:

Main Battle Tanks (MBT) - Approx 100 x Challenger.
Armoured Infantry Fighting Vehicles (AIFV) - Approx 90 x Warrior
Armoured Personnel Carriers (APCs) - Approx 172 x Saxon.
Self Propelled (SP) Artillery - Approx 48 x AS90.
Wheeled Artillery - Approx 18 x Light Gun.
Multi Launch Rocket System (MLRS) - Approx 18 Launchers
Lynx Helicopters armed with TOW missiles - approx 24

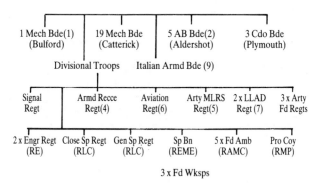

Note: (1) 1 Mechanised Brigade; (2) 5 Airborne Brigade; (3) 3 Commando Brigade a Royal Naval formation is available to support 3(UK) Div if necessary. Details of the organisation of 3 Cdo Bde are given in the Miscellaneous Chapter. 3 Cdo Bde is not under the command of 3 Div; (4) Armoured Reconnaissance Regiment; (5) Artillery Regiment with Multi Launch Rocket System; (6) Army Air Corps Regiment with Lynx & Gazelle; (7) Air Defence Regiments with Rapier and

Javelin/Starstreak missiles;(8) The composition of this division with a lightly armed parachute brigade plus a marine commando brigade allows the UK MOD to retain a balanced force for out of NATO area operations should that become necessary (9) Under Allied Rapid Reaction Corps framework agreements this division could be reinforced by an Italian Armoured Brigade (Ariete).

3 (UK) Division - Mechanised Brigade Organisation

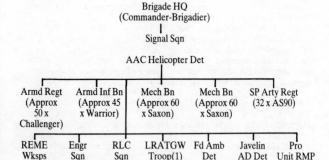

Note: (1) Long Range Anti-Tank Guided Weapons-Currently Striker/Swingfire.

3 (UK) Division - 5 Airborne Brigade Organisation

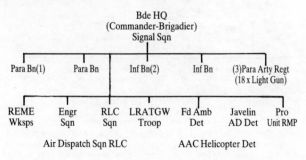

Note: (1) Parachute Battalion ; (2) Infantry Battalion; (3) It is possible that under this new organisation the Para Arty Regt may receive an extra battery bringing the total of Light Guns to 24; (4) The Logistic elements come under the overall command of 5 AB Bde Logistics Bn.

Allied Command Europe Mobile Force Land AMF(L) Contingent

This contingent is the UK's contribution to the Allied Command Europe Mobile Force (AMF) which is tasked with the reinforcement of the flanks of NATO. On mobilisation operations would probably take place in either Norway or Turkey and the UK MOD has recently stated that the UK's contribution to the AMF will be retained. The AMF is a Brigade+ NATO formation with about 6,000 men and 1,500 vehicles.

In 1995 the UK contingent on an AMF(L) exercise in Norway included 1 x Infantry Bn, 1 x Armoured Sqn, 1 Locating Bty, 1 x Artillery Bty, 1 x Signals Sqn, 1 x Engineer Field Troop, 1 x Army Air Corps Flight, 1 x Transport Sqn, 1 x Ordnance Company, REME Workshop, Field Ambulance detachment and an Intelligence section. The overall personnel total was probably in the region of 1500 men.

24 Airmobile Brigade (24 Airmob Bde)

On 1 April 1988, 24 Infantry Brigade based at Catterick in North Yorkshire, was redesignated 24 Airmobile Brigade with the role of acting as a flexible, high speed anti-tank reserve force. The Brigade moved to Colchester in March 1993, and was enhanced considerably under the "Options for Change" review. 24 Airmob Bde now forms part of the Multi National Division - Central (MND(C)) which was formed officially on 1 April 1994. The MND(C) also comprises 31 German Luftlande Brigade, a Belgian Paracommando Brigade and 11 Netherlands Airmobile Brigade, giving the Division the reach, speed and flexibility it will require to be part of the ARRC's most mobile formation.

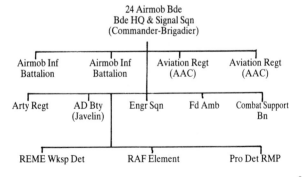

Note: (1) Support helicopters are provided by the RAF and the Brigade would normally expect to operate with 18 x Chinook and 18 x Puma. An airmobile infantry battalion can be moved by 20 x Chinook equivalents. (2) Each airmobile infantry battalion is equipped with 42 x Milan firing posts - a total of 84 within the Brigade.(3) By late 1995 plus we believe that 3 Regt Army Air Corps and 4 Regt Army Air Corps both of whom will be based at RAF Wattisham will support 24 Airmob Bde.

Northern Ireland

The military presence in support of the civilian authorities in Northern Ireland is controlled by HQ Northern Ireland (HQNI) which is located at Lisburn, just outside Belfast.

HQNI has three brigades under command. These brigades, 39 Bde, 8 Bde and 3 Bde are responsible for counter terrorist operations in support of the Royal Ulster Constabulary (RUC). Under the operational command of these (during late 1994) brigades were:

6 x Resident Infantry Battalions
4/5 x Infantry Battalions on short 6 month tours
2 x RA/RAC Regiments on short 6 month tours
1 x Engineer Regiment
1 x Royal Signals Regiment
1 x Army Air Corps Regiment
6 x Home Service Battalions of the Royal Irish Regiment
1 x RLC Logistic Support Regiment
1 x REME Workshop
1 x Military Hospital manned by the Army Medical Services
1 x Prison Guard Force of Squadron/Battery strength
RAF: 1 x Wessex Squadron
1 x Puma Squadron
1 x RAF Regiment Squadron

Navy: 4 x Ships
2 x Launches

During late 1994 there were approximately 12,000 regular soldiers and around 5,600 Royal Irish Regiment Home Service soldiers stationed in the Province (a high percentage on detachment from units either permanently stationed in Germany or the remainder of the UK Military Districts) making a total of approximately 17,500 soldiers available for security duties. In addition there are approximately 240 Royal Naval and 1,100 Royal Air Force personnel stationed in the Province.

Ulster Statistics
The last year for which comprehensive statistics are available was 1992.

	1992	1980
Deaths (Regular Army)	4	8
Deaths (Royal Irish)	2	8
Bombs neutralised	149	120
Explosives neutralised	4,142 Kgs	2,905 Kgs
Used in explosions	7,206 Kgs (est)	4,108 Kgs
Explosives found	2,167 Kgs	821 Kgs
Weapons found	243	203
Ammunition found	29,131 rounds	28,078 rounds

Overseas Garrisons

Brunei:
900 personnel
1 Gurkha Infantry Battalion
Jungle Warfare Training School
1 Helicopter Flight

Cyprus:
3,500 personnel
2 Infantry Battalions
1 Armoured Recce Squadron
1 Engineer Support Squadron
1 Helicopter Flight
1 Signals Regiment
With UNFICYP (United Nations Force in Cyprus)
1 Roulement Regiment - Infantry Role.
1 Helicopter Flight
1 Logistic Support Regiment
1 Armd Recce Squadron

Falkland
Islands:
500 men & women (approx)
1 Infantry Company Group
1 Engineer Squadron
1 Signals Unit
1 Logistics Group
Plus RAF and RN Units.

Gibraltar:
129 regular soldiers approx
1 Engineer Squadron (-)
The Gibraltar Regiment (Reserve Unit)

Hong Kong:
3,000 personnel (Total includes RAF & RN)
1 Gurkha Infantry Battalion

	1 Helicopter Squadron (-)
	Gurkha Engineer Regiment
	Gurkha Signal Regiment
	Gurkha Transport Regiment
	Gurkha Training Depot
Former	3,500 Approx
Yugoslavia:	1 x Armoured Infantry Bn +
	1 x Mechanised Infantry Bn
	2 x Light Armoured Squadrons
	1 x Engineer Regiment (-)
	1 x Logistics Battalion
	1 x National Headquarters
	1 x Medical Battalion
	1 x Cymbeline Troop
	1 x Army Air Corps Squadron
	1 x RAF Support Helicopter Detachment
Other	Approx 1,200 men in about 26 countries including
Locations:	Brunei, Botswana, Egypt, Gambia, Ghana, Mauritius,
	Namibia, Nigeria, Oman, Qatar, Saudi Arabia, Sudan,
	Swaziland, United Arab Emirates, Uganda, Zimbabwe, Kenya
	and Canada.

Reserve Forces

The Regular Army Reserve

Every Officer or soldier completing a regular engagement has a liability for reserve service depending on the contract that he or she signed at the beginning of their regular engagement. A typical enlistment contract would state that regular service would be for a term of 9/22, meaning 9 years service with the colours and a remaining 13 years on the Regular Army Reserve to make up the 22 years of the contract. Officers remain on the reserve list until they are 55 years old.

On mobilisation the 192,500 men and women who are at present on the reserve list would be recalled for colour service, and in theory the size of the army would almost triple overnight. However, many of these reservists would have left the regular forces some time ago, and it is generally acknowledged that a man who has been out of the service for five years or more would not be ready for front line duty. Equipment and procedures change fast, and many reservists would require extensive retraining before being posted to active units.

An examination of the latest government figures show that about 110,000 men and women have left the Regular Army during the past 5 years, and these reservists would probably be used to bring front line units up to war establishment.

The Territorial Army (TA)

At the beginning of 1995 the TA consisted of approximately 60,000 personnel. On mobilisation, the TA would be expected to field a significant number of major units that would be used for the defence of the UK and the reinforcement of the ARRC in Germany. Many of these units have operational tasks on that are just as demanding as those undertaken by regular soldiers and TA units earmarked for service in Germany have the same equipment as the regulars that they will support. A major effort is made to ensure that TA soldiers are trained to the highest standards.

TA soldiers are part-timers who devote much of their leisure to soldiering and although the standards in the TA vary from unit to unit, the overall standard is surprisingly high; with many units proving to be more than a match for their regular counterparts.

Each member of the TA has to complete 44 training days a year of which 15 days are spent at an annual camp or on a military base. For a full day's service TA soldiers are paid in line with regular rates of pay, and special payments are made for an evening's attendance at the local drill hall. All members of the TA receive an annual tax free cash payment known as "the bounty" which increases with each year of service. In 1989 "the bounty" for a TA soldier who had completed 3 years service was £600.

Current plans appear to place a large part of the defence of the mainland UK in the hands of the TA. TA soldiers have been assigned national defence roles such as, guarding vital installations, undertaking reconnaissance and early warning, providing communications and damage control. In early 1995 a composite TA platoon served alongside the regular infantry component of the Falkland Islands garrison, and if this experiment is successful we believe that there will be a dramatic extension in the scheme. TA Soldiers on short term contracts could prove to be valuable additions to regular units where manpower is at a premium.

Strength of Territorial Army (1 January 1995)

Armour	5 Regiments
Royal Artillery	6 Regiments (1)
Royal Engineers	9 Regiments
Infantry	36 Battalions
Special Air Service	2 Regiments
Signals	11 Regiments
Equipment Support	4 Battalions
Logistics	11 Regiments

| Medical | 23 Hospitals/Field Ambulances |
| Special Air Service | 2 Regiments |

Notes: (1) Includes Honourable Artillery Company (HAC).

During 1994 there were rumours of deep cuts to be made in the TA as part of the "Defence Costs Study". When the report was finally published at the end of 1994 there was great relief in military circles that large scale cuts in personnel numbers were not to be made. Indeed it is arguable that the TA has probably been given an enhanced role as a general reserve for the Regular Army, providing individual or formed unit reinforcements world-wide during peace a well as war. The report points to a much greater use of the TA in the years ahead.

The main provisions of the report are as follows:

a. The TA personnel establishment figure will be reduced to 59,000 by April 1997.

b. The Royal Yeomanry has been given the role of a NBC Defence Regiment with a new squadron to be formed in Hampshire and Berkshire. This new squadron will make the regiment up to four squadrons with the other three squadrons coming from Leicestershire, Surrey and Wiltshire.

c. The 8th Battalion of the Light Infantry will take over the Royal Yeomanry's task in the national defence reconnaissance role. The three rifle companies will convert to becoming three reconnaissance companies.

d. Changes in the numbers of company/squadron sized units will be as follows:

	Current Total	New Total
Infantry Companies	109	87
Royal Armoured Corps	17	22
Royal Logistic Corps	69	86
Adjutant General's Corps	10	11
REME	13	16

e. Four infantry battalions will be reorganised as fire support battalions available for deployment in support of all infantry battalions both regular and TA. These fire support battalions will have a total strength of 336 and be organised into two heavy weapons companies, each of three platoons - 81mm mortar, Milan anti-tank and heavy machine gun platoons. The infantry battalions that will become fire support battalions are:

3rd Bn The Prince of Wales's Own Regiment of Yorkshire
3rd Bn The Cheshire Regiment
5th Bn The Royal Green Jackets

51st Highland Volunteers

These fire support battalions will be assigned to the ARRC together with a further eight infantry battalions that will also be available to this NATO formation. ARRC TA infantry battalions will lose their support weapons platoons and each battalion will have three rifle companies.

f. The 1st and 2nd Battalions of the Wessex Regiment will merge and the Royal Anglian TA will reduce to two battalions with the disbanded battalion providing the core of a new transport regiment.

g. Two Royal Signals brigade national communications units will be formed to support Land Command.

h. An armoured delivery regiment will be raised in Dorset and an independent combat service support squadron will be formed.

i. The Royal Engineers will form a Civil Affairs Group that will provide teams capable of supporting transport, public health, utilities and law and order.

Note: The TA Order of Battle in Chapter 10 reflects the organisation at the end of 1994. The next edition of this guide will deal with the new TA organisation in greater depth as the situation becomes clearer.

CHAPTER 3 - BRITISH FORCES GERMANY

(Situation at 1 Jan 95)

British Forces Germany (BFG) is the composite name given to the British Army, Royal Air Force and supporting civil elements stationed in Germany. The terms British Army of the Rhine (BAOR) and Royal Air Force Germany (RAFG), until recently were the traditional names used to describe the two Service elements of the British Forces stationed in Germany.

For many years following WWII, and as a result of the confrontation between NATO and the former Warsaw Treaty Organisation, the UK Government had stationed four divisions and a considerable part of its Air Force at five airbases in the Federal Republic of Germany. On the whole this level of committment was maintained until 1992 and although these forces appeared to be solely national, they were in fact closely integrated with the NATO Northern Army Group (NORTHAG) and the 2nd Allied Tactical Air Force (2 ATAF).

As a result of political changes in Europe and the UK Government's "Options for Change" programme, the British Army's presence in Germany will be reduced to a District Headquarters - United Kingdom Support Command (Germany) (UKSC-(G)) and one armoured division of three armoured brigades (1 (UK) Armd Div) all under the direct command of HQ Land Command at Wilton in the UK from 1 April 1995. The RAF presence has been concentrated on a Group Headquarters and two airbases (to be reduced to 1 in 1999).

British Army in Germany - Major Headquarters

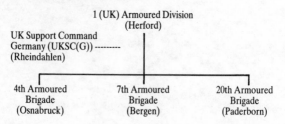

UKSC (G)

Is a District Headquarters commanded by a Major-General responsible for the infrastructure support to all UK Service Personnel (Army and RAF), civilian staff and dependents in Europe and the focal point for all Anglo German dealings. UKSC (G) also commands all those British troops in Germany not integral to 1 (UK) Armoured Division.

1 (UK) Armoured Division is assigned to SACEUR's ARRC (Allied Command Europe Rapid Reaction Corps), as are both 3 (UK) Mechanised Division and 24 Airmobile Brigade in the UK.

UK Force Levels in Germany

Army	April 1992	April 1995
Army Personnel	59,080	26,250
Army Barracks & Facilities	134	46
Main Battle Tanks	657	300
Tracked Vehicles	3,710	1,492
Army Helicopters	123	39

RAF		
RAF Personnel	12,000	6,290
RAF Airfields	5	2
RAF Aircraft	170	78

Miscellaneous Figures		
Hospitals	5	2
Children's Schools	76	39
Local Civilian Staff	19,000	10,700
Army Family Quarters	35,000	17,600
RAF Family Quarters	6,987	3,727

Before examining the composition of BFG it would be helpful to look at the current NATO Command Structure in Europe.

NATO Command Structure

Following re-organisations taking effect from 1 July 1993, NATO was reorganised from three into two major Commands. The first is ACLANT (Allied Command Atlantic) with headquarters at Norfolk, Virginia (USA) and the second is ACE (Allied Command Europe), with its headquarters at Mons in Belgium.

Operations in the European area, in which the United Kingdom would participate will almost certainly be as part of a NATO force under the command and control of Allied Command Europe (ACE). The current Supreme Allied Commander Europe is General George A Joulwan of the United States Army who replaced General John M Shalikashvili on the 4th of October 1993. The new organisation of Allied Command Europe is as follows:

Allied Command Europe

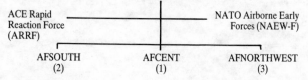

SHAPE
(Supreme Headquarters Allied Powers Europe)
Mons - Belgium

SACEUR
(Supreme Allied Commander Europe)
General George A Joulwan - US Army

ACE Rapid Reaction Force (ARRF)

NATO Airborne Early Forces (NAEW-F)

| AFSOUTH (2) | AFCENT (1) | AFNORTHWEST (3) |

Notes:

(1) AFCENT - Allied Forces Central Europe with headquartes at Brunssum in the Netherlands and with overall responsibility for military operations in Central Europe. AFCENT is further subdivided into three subordinate commands - see next diagram.

(2) AFSOUTH - Allied Forces Southern Europe, with headquarters at Naples in Italy and responsible for military operations in the area of Turkey, Greece and Italy.

(3) AFNORTHWEST - Allied Forces North-western Europe, with headquarters at High Wycombe in the UK. This new headquarters, became operational on 1 July 1994 and is responsible for operations in Norway, the UK, and the maritime area between the two countries. The Chief of Staff (Dec 1994) is Lieutenant General Ola Aabakken of the Norwegian Army.

(4) ARRF - Allied Rapid Reaction Forces include the ARRC (Allied Command Europe Rapid Reaction Corps) to which the majority of the British Army Units under NATO command are assigned. In war it is very possible that UK Forces could find themselves under the command of AFCENT (Allied Forces Central European Theatre) and following the most recent re-organisation the composition of AFCENT is as follows:

AFCENT - Allied Forces Central Europe

AFCENT
Commander-in-Chief
Allied Forces Central Europe
(CINCENT)
General H von Ondarza
German Army
HQ Brunssum - Netherlands

AIRCENT (1)	LANDCENT (2)	BALTAP
Commander	Commander	Commander
Allied Air Forces	Allied Land Forces	Allied Forces Baltic
Central Europe	Central Europe	Approaches
General RB Oaks USAF	General MJ Wilmink	Lt General KGH Hillingsoe
HQ Ramstein - Germany	Netherlands Army	Danish Army
	HQ Heidelberg - Germany	HQ Karup - Denmark

Note:

(1) AIRCENT is now responsible for all air forces in the AFCENT region.
(2) As an example, the LANDCENT HQ Staff consists of 159 Officers, 149
Non-commissioned Officers and Other Ranks and 15 NATO civilians - a total of
323 headquarters personnel. With Direct Support Units included the total is 744,
and with the supporting Signal Unit the personnel figure is approximately 2,500.
(3) The AFCENT operational area includes Northern Germany and Denmark,
extending 800 kms to the south as far as the Swiss and Austrian borders.

The Allied Command Europe Rapid Reaction Corps (ARRC)

NATO's latest strategic planning concept, which was initiated by the NATO
Defence Planning Committee in May 1991 and confirmed during November 1991,
called for the creation of Rapid Reaction Forces to meet the requirements of future
challenges within the alliance, whilst restructuring and reductions in national
defence forces are going ahead. The ARRC provides the Supreme Allied
Commander Europe with a multinational corps in which forward elements can be
ready to deploy in Western Europe within 14 days.
Currently the ARRC trains for missions across the spectrum of operations from
deterrence and crisis management to regional conflict. The formation has to be
prepared to undertake Peace Support Operations - both peacekeeping and
peacemaking.
Belgium, Canada, Denmark, Germany, Greece, Italy, The Netherlands, Norway,
Portugal, Spain, Turkey, the United Kingdom and the United States all contribute
to the Corps. Ten divisions are assigned to the ARRC and up to four of them could
be placed under command for any specific operation. These divisions range from
heavily armoured formations to lighter air portable units more suited to

mountainous or difficult terrain. Some of these formations are National Divisions, some are Framework Divisions, where one nation takes the lead and another contributes, and two are Multinational Divisions where the member nations provide an equal share of the command, staff and combat forces.

The headquarters of the ARRC is fully multinational and is based at Rheindahlen, near Monchengladbach in Germany. The ARRC Commander is a British 3 Star General (from December 1994 - Lt General Michael Walker), the Deputy Commander is an Italian 2 Star General and the Chief of Staff is a British 2 Star General. The Headquarters is approximately 1,000 strong, of which British personnel comprise about 50%. During October 1994 the Headquarters of the ARRC deployed outside Germany for the first time when the formation took part in Exercise Chinese Eye in Denmark. The ARRC becomes operational during early 1995.

Outline Composition of the ARRC (ACE Rapid Reaction Corps)

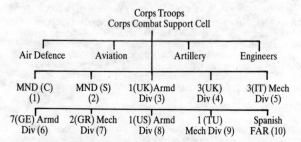

Notes: (1) MND(C) - Multinational Division - Central; (2) Multinational Division - South (3) Resident in Germany (4) Resident in the UK (5) IT - Italy (6) GE - Germany (7) GR - Greece (8) US - United States (9) TU - Turkish (10) FAR - Rapid Action Force.

In peace, the headquarters of the ARRC and the two Multinational Divisions are under the command of SACEUR, but the remaining divisions and units only come under SACEUR's operational control after being deployed.

The operational organisation, composition and size of the ARRC would depend on the type of crisis, area of crisis, its political significance, and the capabilities and availability of lift assets, the distances to be covered and the infrastructure capabilities of the nation receiving assistance. It is considered that a four-division ARRC would be the maximum employment structure.

The main British contribution to the ARRC is 1 (UK) Armoured Division that is stationed in Germany. There are also a considerable number of British personnel in both the ARRC Corps HQ and Corps Troops. In addition, in times of tension 3(UK) Div and 24 Airmobile Bde could take their place in the ARRC's order of battle. In total, we believe that if the need arises some 55,000 British Regular soldiers could be assigned to the ARRC (23,000 resident in Germany) together with substantial numbers of Regular Army Reservists and formed TA Units.

The mission statement of the ARRC is as follows:

"Be prepared to deploy ARRC forces of corps troops and up to four divisions on military operations in support of SACEUR's crisis management options".

ARRC Groupings

Composition of the Multinational Division (Central) - MND(C)

Composition of the Multinational Division (South) - MND(S)

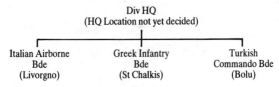

Composition of the 1st (UK) Armoured Division

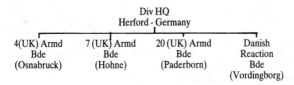

Composition of the 3rd (UK) Mechanised Division

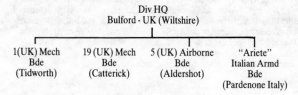

Div HQ
Bulford - UK (Wiltshire)

| 1 (UK) Mech Bde (Tidworth) | 19 (UK) Mech Bde (Catterick) | 5 (UK) Airborne Bde (Aldershot) | "Ariete" Italian Armd Bde (Pardenone Italy) |

Composition of the 3rd Italian Mechanised Division

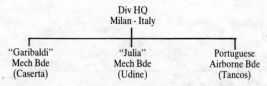

Div HQ
Milan - Italy

| "Garibaldi" Mech Bde (Caserta) | "Julia" Mech Bde (Udine) | Portuguese Airborne Bde (Tancos) |

Composition of the 7th German Panzer Division

Div HQ
Dusseldorf - Germany

| 21 (GE) Armd Bde (Augustdorf) | 9 (GE) Armd Bde (Munster) |

Composition of the 2nd Greek Mechanised Division

Div HQ
Edessa - Northern Greece

| 33 (GR) Mech Bde (Polikastru) | Greek Mech Bde (Thessaloniki) | Bde to be allocated as required. |

Note: Other NATO nations could be invited to contribute a similar brigade to act as the third brigade within this divisional framework structure.

Composition of the 1st United States Armoured Division

Composition of the 1st Turkish Mechanised Division

Composition of the Spanish FAR Contingent
(Fuerza De Accion Rapida)

Note: The Spanish FAR equates roughly to the size of a conventional division.

(Composition of 1(UK) Armoured Division)

1 (UK) Armoured Division has its headquarters at Herford in Germany (about 50kms from Hanover) and the three Armoured Brigades under command are located at Osnabruck, Bergen-Hohne and Paderborn.

Div HQ
(Commander- Major General)
(Herford)

1 x Signal Regiment
1 x Armd Recce Regt
1 x Aviation Regt

4 Armoured Brigade (1) (Osnabruck)	7 Armoured Brigade (Bergen)	20 Armoured Brigade (Paderborn)	Divisional Troops	DAG(2) 3 x Fd Regts 1 x LLAD Regt 1 x MLRS Regt(3)

4 x Engineer Regts (RE)	2 x Logistic Regts (RLC)	3 x Support Bns (REME)	3 x Fd Amb (RAMC)	Pro Coy (RMP)

The divisional totals probably resemble the following:

297 x Challenger MBT
273 x Warrior AIFV & 710 A_FV 432
96 x AS 90 Guns and 18 x MLRS
24 x AVLB & 54 AAC Helicopters

Note: (1) Current plans appear to be for all three armoured brigades to have an identical organisation. (2) DAG (Divisional Artillery Group) This DAG could be reinforced by Rapier Air Defence and MLRS units from the UK as necessary. (3) The MLRS Regiment currently stationed in Germany is returning to the UK in late 1995. (4) Personnel total is about 19,000.

This Division could provide the Headquarters (HQs) for 12 Battlegroups.

It is probable that in the event of hostilities considerable numbers of officers and soldiers from the Territorial Army (TA) would be used to reinforce an armoured division such as this. These reinforcements would consist of individuals, drafts of specialists, or by properly formed TA units varying in size from Mobile Bath Units of 20 men, to Major Units over 500 strong. For example the UK MOD recently announced that eight TA infantry battalions had a role that entailed possible support for the ARRC.

The Armoured Brigade

The following diagram illustrates the possible composition of an Armoured Brigade in 1(UK) Armd Div on operations.

Armd Bde
HQ
(Commander-Brigadier)
Signal Sqn

Armd Regt(1)	Armd Inf Bn (2)	Armd Regt	Armd Inf Bn	Arty Regt(3)
Engr(4) Regt	RLC Sqn(5)	Pro Det RMP	Fd Amb RAMC	REME Wksp

Totals: 100 x Challenger MBT (Possibly)
      90 x Warrior AIFV
      80 x AFV 432 APC 32 x AS 90 SP Gun
      Approx 4,500 men

Notes: (1) Armoured Regiment with approx 50 Challenger MBT; (2) Armoured Inf Battalion with approx 60 x Warrior (with rifle coys) and approx 40 x FV432; (3) Artillery Regiment with 32 AS90 SP Guns; (4) Engineer Regiment with an HQ Sqn, Armd Engr Sqn, Mechanised Field Sqn and possibly additional resources dependent upon task; (5) Brigade Support Squadron RLC with approximately 60 -70 trucks; (6) Depending upon task the Brigade could expect to be reinforced with Medium Reconnaissance, Aviation and Air Defence Units.

This Brigade could provide the HQs for 4 Battlegroups

The Battlegroup

A division usually consists of 3 brigades. These brigades are further sub-divided into smaller formations known as battlegroups. The Batlegroup is the basic building brick of the fighting formations.

A battlegroup is commanded by a Lieutenant Colonel and the infantry battalion or armoured regiment that he commands provides the command and staff element of the formation. The battlegroup is then structured according to task, with the correct mix of infantry, armour and supporting arms.

The battlegroup organisation is very flexible and the units assigned can be quickly regrouped to cope with a change in the threat. A typical battlegroup fighting a defensive battle , might be composed of one armoured squadron and two armoured infantry companies, containing about 600 men, 12 tanks and about 80 armoured personnel carriers.

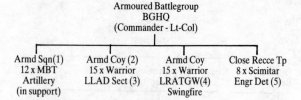

Armoured Battlegroup
BGHQ
(Commander - Lt-Col)

Armd Sqn(1)	Armd Coy (2)	Armd Coy	Close Recce Tp
12 x MBT	15 x Warrior	15 x Warrior	8 x Scimitar
Artillery	LLAD Sect (3)	LRATGW(4)	Engr Det (5)
(in support)		Swingfire	

Mortars (in support)

(1) Armoured Squadron
(2) Armoured Infantry Company
(3) LLAD-Low Level Air Defence - Javelin
(4) LRATGW - Long Range Anti Tank Guided Weapon- Swingfire.
(5) Engineer Detachment - The number of battlegroups in a division and a brigade could vary according to the task the formation has been given. As a general rule you could expect a division to have as many as 12 battlegroups and a brigade to have up to 4. The diagram shows a possible organisation for an armoured battlegroup in either 1(UK) Armd Div or 3(UK) Div.

Company/Squadron Groups

Each battlegroup will operate with smaller organisations called squadron or company groups. These are commanded by a Major, and will be allocated tanks, armoured personnel carriers and supporting elements depending upon the aim of the formation. Supporting elements such as air defence, anti-tank missiles, fire support and engineer expertise ensure that the company/squadron group is a balanced all arms grouping, tailored specifically for the task. In general a battlegroup similar to the one in the previous diagram could be expected to form 3 company groups.

Expect a Company Group organisation to resemble the following diagram:

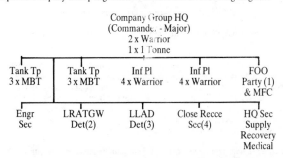

Company Group HQ
(Commander - Major)
2 x Warrior
1 x 1 Tonne

Tank Tp	Tank Tp	Inf Pl	Inf Pl	FOO
3 x MBT	3 x MBT	4 x Warrior	4 x Warrior	Party (1)
				& MFC

Engr	LRATGW	LLAD	Close Recce	HQ Sec
Sec	Det(2)	Det(3)	Sec(4)	Supply
				Recovery
				Medical

Notes: (1) Forward Observation Officer (FOO - usually a Captain) with his party from the Royal Artillery. This FOO will be in direct communication with the Artillery Fire Direction Centre. The MFC is usually a sergeant from an infantry battalion mortar platoon who may have up to six mortar tubes on call. In most Combat Teams both the FOO and MFC will travel in close proximity to the Combat Team Commander; (2) Possibly 2 x Striker with Swingfire; (3) Possibly 2 x Spartan with Javelin; (4) Possibly 2 x Scimitar.

CHAPTER 4 - CAVALRY

"If you want to have a good time - Join the Cavalry".

JEB Stuart - Confederate Cavalry Leader - American Civil War.

Apart from the Royal Tank Regiment, which was formed in the First World War with the specific task of fighting in armoured vehicles, tank forces in the British Army are provided by the regiments which formed the cavalry element of the pre-mechanised era. Following the "Options for Change" restructuring in January 1995 there are 11 regular regiments and 5 TA armoured reconnaisance regiments. One of these regiments is The Household Cavalry and the remaining regiments are known collectively as The Royal Armoured Corps (RAC).

Of these 11 regular armoured regiments, 7 are stationed in Germany with 1 (UK) Armoured Division, and of these 7 regiments in 1 (UK) Armoured Division - 6 are equipped with Challenger main battle tanks, and the 7th is an armoured reconnaissance regiment equipped with a mix of Scimitar, Striker and Spartan.

In the UK there are 2 regular armoured regiments equipped with Challenger MBT stationed in Tidworth and Catterick. Both of these regiments are under the operational command of 3 (UK) Division that has a role in support of the ARRC. There is also 1 regular armoured reconnaissance regiment stationed in the UK also under the operational command of 3 (UK) Division. An armoured training regiment is based at the RAC Training Centre located at Bovington in Dorset. In addition to these armoured forces the Household Cavalry Mounted Regiment is stationed in London and provides mounted troops for ceremonial duties.

The Territorial Army has 5 Yeomanry Regiments and an independent squadron. These units provide 1 armoured reconnaissance regiment for the reinforcement of the ARRC and 4 national defence regiments with a reconnaissance role.

During late 1994 the UK MOD announced the formation of the British Army's first Nuclear, Biological and Chemical Defence Regiment (NBC). During the period 1995 to 1997 one of the Territorial Army's Yeomanry Regiments - The Royal Yeomanry will convert from its current role as a national defence reconnaissance regiment and as equipment becomes available adopt the new role. In the longer term the Royal Yeomanry will support all existing plans for NBC defence throughout the British Army and could be used to support action following radiological accidents and chemical spills.The core element of this new regiment will be the 11 x Fuchs reconnaissance vehicles that were supplied to the British Army during the Gulf War. These 11 vehicles will form one squadron, with another two squadrons mounted in wheeled vehicles. All three squadrons will be equipped with the joint US/UK Integrated Biological Detection System

(IBDS) the British version of which is currently under development at the Chemical Defence Establishment at Porton Down in Wiltshire.

In early July 1991 the UK MOD announced the purchase of 127 Vickers Defence Systems Challenger 2 main battle tanks. Vickers Defence Systems won the £500 million contract against intense competition from the French Leclerc, German Leopard 2 (Improved) and the US M1A2 Abrams. The Challenger 2 MBT unit price is believed to be in the region of £2.5 million pounds and defence industry sources suggest that this price was considerably cheaper than that of the French Leclerc or the German Leopard 2. In July 1994 the UK Secretary of State for Defence announced the purchase of a further 259 Challenger 2 bringing the total to 386, and allowing for the complete UK MBT fleet to be upgraded to the Challenger 2 standard.

At the same time it was announced that in future British armoured regiments operating Challenger 2 MBT would reduce from regiments with 50 main battle tanks organised in four squadrons to a new organisation of 38 tanks with three squadrons. This will allow for six Challenger 2 regiments in Germany, two in the UK, a training regiment at Bovington and a war maintenance reserve (WMR) of approximately 50 tanks.

The Royal Scots Dragoon Guards will take delivery of the first production models of the Challenger 2 in July 1995 and the Regiment will move from Catterick to Germany during late 1995 as the first regiment fully equipped with the new tank.

At the time of writing the long term future of the MBT in its present form is uncertain, and although the most dedicated armoured soldier will still insist that the tank is the most effective anti-tank weapon on the battlefield, others would disagree. The supremacy of armour on the modern battlefield is being challenged by anti-tank helicopters such as the Russian Havoc and US Apache. Helicopters which travel at speeds of up to 300 kph, carrying missiles with ranges of up to 5,000+ metres, threaten the flanks of armoured formations that might have a top speed of 80 kph and effective gun ranges of 2,000 metres. On the ground the infantry can defend themselves with portable missile systems such as the Soviet Spigot, European Milan and US TOW, while third generation "fire and forget" weapons such as Trigat that are shortly to enter service will further enhance defences. Missiles such as these, with ranges in excess of 2,000 metres, and the ability to penetrate over 350mm of armour, contribute to making the modern battlefield a difficult environment for armour.

Syrian experience in the Lebanon during the 1982 war, when over 400 Soviet manufactured Syrian T-62 and T-72's were destroyed by the Israelis using a combination of aircraft, attack helicopters and ground based TOW missiles, would serve to underline this belief. We feel that recent experience in the Gulf has added more weight to the argument in favour of the attack helicopter and do not believe that the current trend in up-armouring main battle tanks will do anything more than obtain a short breathing space for armour, before the next round of improvements in anti-tank weapons appear.

The correct answer to this problem would be to have large numbers of MBT, attack helicopters and ground based anti-armour systems, but it is unrealistic to expect that a small nation with expensive world-wide commitments can afford this luxury. Up to now the British Defence Establishment appears to have made armour its highest priority, but there are now clear signs which suggest that in the longer term thinking may be slowly moving in the direction of a heliborne missile anti-tank defensive system. We see the establishment of 24 Airmobile Brigade and the creation of a sixth Army Air Corps Regiment as evidence of a gradual shift in emphasis in favour of the anti-tank helicopter solution.

However, we do not believe that the Main Battle Tank is redundant on the modern battlefield. Armour will almost certainly have a major military role to play for many years to come and we predict that during the early part of the next century armoured formations will remain an essential part of any military force. We are at the beginning of a time of great military change, and the only military certainty that we can see on the horizon is for the continuing need to hold or capture ground. This requirement alone should ensure the survival of armoured formations, but the size of these formations will almost certainly be greatly reduced, and organisations and tactics could be very different from those which are in use today.

For the longer term the "crystal ball" appears to be clearing a little. While we are reasonably certain of a reduction in the numbers of main battle tanks in most national inventories, the manouverable light armoured vehicle, capable of operating in a 24 hour battlefield scenario and possibly acting as a command and control unit (electronic mother station/digital relay) for smaller mobile sub units is beginning to look like a priority option. The UK Verdi and Tracer programmes appear to be coming together to provide such an option and digitisation of the future battlefield may well see large numbers of these vehicles in service during the early part of the new century.

Armoured Regiment Wiring Diagram

The following diagram shows the current structure of an Armoured Regiment equipped with Challenger 1. Regiments equipped with Challenger 2 will only have three "sabre" squadrons and a total of 38 tanks.

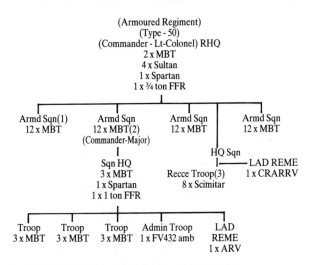

(Armoured Regiment)
(Type - 50)
(Commander - Lt-Colonel) RHQ
2 x MBT
4 x Sultan
1 x Spartan
1 x ¾ ton FFR

Armd Sqn(1)
12 x MBT

Armd Sqn
12 x MBT(2)
(Commander-Major)

Sqn HQ
3 x MBT
1 x Spartan
1 x 1 ton FFR

Armd Sqn
12 x MBT

Armd Sqn
12 x MBT

HQ Sqn ——— LAD REME
1 x CRARRV

Recce Troop(3)
8 x Scimitar

Troop
3 x MBT

Troop
3 x MBT

Troop
3 x MBT

Admin Troop
1 x FV432 amb

LAD REME
1 x ARV

Totals: 50 x MBT (Challenger 1), 8 x Scimitar, 5 x ARV, 558 men.

Notes: (1) Armoured Squadron; (2) Main Battle Tank; (3) We believe that this recce troop of 8 x Scimitar is normally held in HQ Sqn but on operations comes under the direct control of the commanding officer; (4) By late 1993 all 6 regiments in Germany with 1(UK) Armd Div were equipped with Challenger. (5) The basic building brick of the Tank Regiment is the Tank Troop of 12 men and three tanks. The commander of this troop will probably be a Lt or 2/Lt aged between 20 or 23 and the second-in-command will usually be a sergeant who commands his own tank. The remaining tank in the troop will be commanded by a senior corporal; (6) A Challenger tank has a crew of 4 - Commander, Driver, Gunner and Loader/Operator.

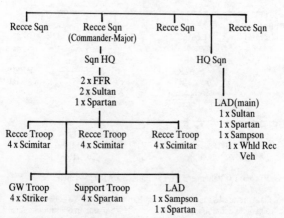

Armoured Reconnaissance Regiment
(Commander - Lt-Colonel)

RHQ
4 x Sultan
3 x Spartan
2 x FFR

Recce Sqn | Recce Sqn (Commander-Major) | Recce Sqn | Recce Sqn

Sqn HQ

2 x FFR
2 x Sultan
1 x Spartan

HQ Sqn

LAD(main)
1 x Sultan
1 x Spartan
1 x Sampson
1 x Whld Rec Veh

Recce Troop
4 x Scimitar

Recce Troop
4 x Scimitar

Recce Troop
4 x Scimitar

GW Troop
4 x Striker

Support Troop
4 x Spartan

LAD
1 x Sampson
1 x Spartan

Totals: 48 x Scimitar, 16 x Striker, 20 x Spartan, Approx 600 men.

At the beginning of 1995 there are 2 regular armoured reconnaissance regiments in the British Order of Battle. One is in Germany with 1(UK) Armd Div and the other is in the UK with 3(UK) Div. Both of these recce regiments have an organisation based on the diagram shown above. TA Yeomanry Recce regiments based in the UK with a national defence role are equipped with open Land Rovers.

Armoured reconnaissance regiments are usually under the direct command of a divisional headquarters and their more usual task in a defensive scenario is to identify the direction and strength of the enemy thrusts, impose maximum delay and damage while allowing main forces to manoeuvre to combat the threat. They would be assisted in such a task by anti-tank helicopters, long range anti-tank missile systems such as Swingfire, and for the action to be successful every engagement will need to be planned as an ambush. In support will be the indirect fire guns of the divisional artillery, and an air defended area (ADA) maintained by Rapier and Javelin air defence missiles.

The basic task of all of these recce regiments is to obtain accurate information about the enemy and ensure that it is passed back through the chain of command as quickly as possible.

Fv 4030/4 Challenger 1

(372 in Operational Service on 1 Jan 1995 - being replaced by Challenger 2 from mid 1995). Armament 1 x 120mm L11A7 gun: 2 x 7.62 Machine Guns: 2 x 5 barrel smoke dischargers: Engine Rolls-Royce CV12: Ammunition Capacity 44 rounds of 120mm: 6000 rounds of 7.62mm: Engine Power 1,200 bhp at 2,300 rpm: Engine Capacity 26.1 litres: Max Road Speed 56kph: Weight loaded 62,000kg: Length Hull 9.87m: Length Gun Forward 11.55m: Height 3.04m: Width 3.42m: Ground Clearance O.5m: Crew 4: Ground Pressure 0.96 kg/cm2: Fording Depth (no prep) 1.07m.

Produced by the Royal Ordnance Factory in Leeds the first Challengers 1 were delivered to the British Army in 1983.

Challenger 1 is a development of the Centurion/Chieftain line which was modified to produce the Shir/Iran 2 originally planned for service with the Iranian forces. After the Iranian Revolution the Shir Iran 2 project was taken over by the British Army and the end result was Challenger later re-designated as Challenger 1.

The main differences between Challenger 1 and its predecessor Chieftain (the MBT that it replaced) are in the engine and armour. The Challenger engine, which produces 1,200bhp at 2,300rpm was far more powerful than the Chieftain engine, and the Chobham Armour carried is believed to give protection from almost all types of anti-tank weapon. Chobham armour is thought to consist of several layers of nylon micromesh, bonded on both sides by sheets of titanium alloy, in addition to several other layers of specialised armour and ceramics. Challenger 1 is believed to have cost about £2 million per vehicle at 1987 prices.

The main armament on all Challenger 1's is currently being upgraded by the installation of the L30 CHARM gun. In addition to firing the existing range of ammunition, this gun fires a new armour piercing fin stabilised discarding sabot round which should be able to defeat the armour on all known MBT's.

The only nation known to be operating Challenger 1 other than the UK is Jordan, where the 274 tanks in service are known as Khalid. The UK also operates approximately 77 Challenger 1 ARRV's and 16 Challenger 1 driver training tanks.

Challenger 2

(386 Challenger 2 on Order) Crew 4; Length Gun Forward 11.55m; Hull Length 8.32m; Height to Turret Roof 2.49m; Width 3.52m; Ground Clearance 0.50m; Combat Weight 62,500 kgs; Main Armament 1 x 120mm L30 CHARM Gun; Ammunition Carried 52 rounds - APFSDS, HESH, Smoke; Secondary Armament Co-axial 7.62mm MG; 7.62mm GPMG Turret Mounted for Air Defence; Ammunition Carried 4000 rounds 7.62mm; Engine CV12TCA 12 cylinder - Auxiliary Engine Perkins 4.108 4 - stroke diesel; Gearbox TN54 epicyclic - 6 forward gears and 2 reverse; Road Speed 56 kph; Cross Country Speed 40 kph; Fuel Capacity 1,797 litres.

In July 1991 the UK MOD announced an order for 127 Challenger 2 MBT and 13 driver training tanks. This initial order was followed in July 1994 by a further contract for 259 vehicles to make a total of 386. This will be enough to equip 8 regiments with the vehicle and allow 82 tanks for training and reserve. A regiment will have 38 tanks in three squadrons. Challenger 2 is manufactured by Vickers Defence Systems and production will be undertaken at their factories in Newcastle-Upon-Tyne and Leeds. At 1995 prices Challenger 2 is believed to cost £2.5 million per vehicle.

Challenger 2 completed its Reliability Growth Trial (RGT) in 1994 and during these trials 3 vehicles were tested over a total of about 285 battlefield days. For the purposes of the trial a battlefield day consisted of:

>   27 kms of Road Travel
>   33 kms of Cross Country Travel
>   Firing 34 Main Armament Rounds
>   Firing 1,000 7.62mm MG rounds
>   16 Hours of Weapon Systems Operation
>   10 Hours of Main Engine Idling
>   3.5 Hours of Main Engine Running - Mobile

Although the hull and automotive parts of the Challenger 2 are based upon that of its predecessor Challenger 1, the new tank incorporates over 150 improvements aimed at increasing reliability and maintainability. The whole of the Challenger 2 turret is of a totally new design and the vehicle has a crew of four - commander, gunner, loader/signaller and driver. The 120mm rifled Royal Ordnance L30 gun fires all current tank ammunition plus the new depleted uranium (DU) round with a stick charge propellant system.

The design of the turret incorporates several of the significant features that Vickers had developed for its Mk 7 MBT (a Vickers turret on a Leopard 2 chassis). The central feature is an entirely new fire control system based on the Ballistic Control System developed by Computing Devices Company (Canada) for the US Army's M1A1 MBT. This second generation computer incorporates dual 32-bit processors with a MIL STD1553B databus and has sufficient growth potential to accept Battlefield Information Control System (BICS) functions and navigation aids (a GPS satnav system). The armour is an uprated version of Challenger 1's Chobham armour.

The first production models of the Challenger 2 are to be taken into service by the Royal Scots Dragoon Guards in mid 1995 and the regiment will be the first to deploy to Germany with the new tank in mid 1995. The actual in service date (ISD) for the vehicle is December 1995 and we would expect to see all 386 Challenger 2's in service with the British Army by the end of the decade.

The only export order so far is an Omani order for 18 x Challenger 2 MBTs, 2 x Driver Training Vehicles and 4 x Challenger Armoured Repair and Recovery Vehicles signed during 1993. However, Vickers Defence Systems have high hopes for the vehicle in the remainder of the world market during the next ten years.

Sabre

As part of the UK MODs CVR(T) rationalisation programme both the tracked Scorpion with its 76mm gun and the wheeled Fox with its 30mm Rarden Cannon were withdrawn from service and a hybrid vehicle - Sabre produced. Essentially Sabre consists of the Scorpion chassis fitted with the turret of a Fox.

In addition to the installation of the manually operated two man Fox turret, extensive modifications have been carried out by 34 Base Workshops at Donnington. These modifications include redesigned smoke grenade dischargers, replacement of the 7.62 MG with a 7.62mm Chain Gun, new light clusters and additional side bins. Domed hatches have also improved headroom for both commander and gunner.

We believe that about 140 Sabre vehicles will be introduced into service.

Fv 102 Striker

(Approx 88 in service) Armament 10 x Swingfire Missiles: 1 x 7.62mm Machine Gun: 2 x 4 barrel smoke dischargers: Engine Jaguar J 60 No.1 Mark 100B: Engine Power 190bhp: Fuel Capacity 350 litres: Max Road Speed 80kph: Road Range 483km: Length 4.8m: Height 2.2m: Width 2.2m: Ground Clearance 0.35m: Ammunition Capacity 3,000 rounds 762: Main Armment Travese 53 degrees left, 55 degrees right.

Striker is one of the family of the CVR(T) vehicles (Combat Vehicle Reconnaissance Tracked) which includes Spartan, Sultan, Samaritan and Scorpion. Striker carries 10 Swingfire anti-tank missiles with a range of up to 4,000 metres. Five of these missiles are carried in bins on top of the vehicle, which can be lowered when the system is not expected to be in action. One significant drawback to the system is the reload operation, which requires a crewman to reload the missile bins from outside the vehicle.

The striker system enables a fast, hard hitting anti-tank missile launch platform to keep up with the latest MBTs. Striker is to be found in the armoured reconnaissance regiment which has a troop of four vehicles in each of its three recce squadrons. Swingfire (cost per missile £7,500) is due for replacement by Trigat LR towards the end of the decade.

Swingfire

Type - Anti Tank Guided Missile; Wire Guided; Command to line of sight: Length of Missile 1.06m: Body Diameter 37.3cm: Warhead Hollow Charge HE: Propellant Solid Fuel: Weight of Missile 37kg: Minimum Range 150m: Maximum Range 4,000m.

Mounted on the AFV 438 the Swingfire missile can be fired from 2 launch containers which can be reloaded from inside the vehicle. There is also a separated sight available which enables the launch vehicle to be hidden in dead ground, and the operator to fire and control the flight of the missile from a position up to 100m away from the launch vehicle.

Trigat LR

Range 5000+ metres: Missile Launch Weight 40 kgs: Length 1.57m: Body Diameter 0.155m.

Trigat is a European collaborative programme which is designed to produce a family of medium and long range, anti-tank missiles for the 1990s and beyond. Trigat LR (Long Range) will probably be the missile that replaces Swingfire in British Service.

Trigat LR is believed to be designed for heliborne or tank destroyer type launch platforms and will have a fully "fire and forget" capability. Present plans are thought to include a launch platform with a raised gantry, which could be elevated to a height of about 6 metres and produce a dramatic increase in the operators field of fire.

Guidance is by automatic passive infra-red CCD homing seeker. Each image recorded is compared to the preceding one by the onboard guidance microprocessor system. This generates flight commands which are transmitted to the aerodynamic flight control surfaces. A tandem HE hollow charge warhead system is fitted with the missile adopting either a terminal dive to attack armoured targets or a direct attack profile to engage low flying or hovering helicopters.

The fire control equipment (computer, display processor, target trackers and alignment processor) evaluates each target acquired by the sensor sight head assembly. This is used for target surveillance, recognition and identification. All the gunner has to do is designate an acquired target for attack. The tracker units allow independent tracking of up to four targets, automatically.

Once the target is designated, an automatic handover sequence is initiated to a missile seeker so that it can lock on. When this is achieved, the missile is fired with the gunner having the option to fire up to four ready-to-fire rounds at individual targets or as a salvo.

We believe that Trigat LR will cost over £50,000 per missile and if this initial estimate is correct, there is little doubt that practice firings will not be an everyday occurrence. The three partners in the Trigat project are France, Germany and the UK with the manufacturer being the Euromissile Dynamics Group. A number of other European Union nations are showing interest in the system.

Fv 107 Scimitar

(290) in service) . Armament 1 x 30mm Rarden L21 Gun: 1 x 7.62mm Machine
Gun: 2 x 4 barrel smoke dischargers: Engine Jaguar J60 No.1 Mark 100B: Engine
Power 190bhp: Fuel Capacity 423 litres: Max Road Speed 80kph: Weight loaded
7,750kg: Length 4.9m: Height 2.096m: Width 2.2m: Ground Clearance 0.35m:
Road Range 644km: Crew 3: Ammunition Capacity 30mm - 160 rounds; 7.62mm -
3,000 rounds: Main Armament Elevation - 10 degrees to + 35 degrees.

Very much the same vehicle as the Scorpion, but with a different gun, the Scimitar
is the mainstay of the Armoured Recce Regiment. The Scimitar is an ideal recce
vehicle, mobile and fast with good communications and excellent viewing
equipment. Recce Platoons belonging to Infantry Battalions stationed in Germany
are also equipped with Scimitar.

Fuchs

(11 In Service) Road Range 800 kms; Crew 2; Operational Weight 17,000 kg;
Length 6.83m; Width 2.98m; Height 2.30m; Road Speed 105 kph; Engine
Mercedes-Benz Model OM-402A V-8 liquid cooled diesel; Armament 1 x 7.62mm
MG; 6 x Smoke Dischargers.

Manufactured by the German company Thyssen-Henschel as the Transporter
Panzer 1 this is an amphibious vehicle with a water speed of 10 kph. During the
Gulf War the UK purchased 11 of the NBC Reconnaissance version of this vehicle
and they will now become the core element of the UKs Nuclear, Biological and
Chemical Defence Regiment being formed by the Royal Yeomanry. For NBC
Defence work the vehicles will be equipped with the joint US/UK Integrated
Biological Detection System (IBDS), the British version of which is currently under
development at the Chemical Defence Establishment at Porton Down in Wiltshire.

Approximately 1,000 Transporter Panzer 1 vehicles are in service with the German Army in 7 basic roles. The NBC version is also in service with the USA (60), Israel (8), Turkey (4) and the Netherlands (6).

Challenger Armoured Repair and Recovery Vehicle (ARRV)

(80 In Service) Crew 3; Length 9.59m; Operating Width 3.62m; Height 3.005m; Ground Clearance 0.5m; Combat Weight 62,000kg; Max Road Speed 59 kph; Cross Country Speed 35 kph; Fording 1.07m; Trench Crossing 2.3m; Crane - Max Lift 6,500kg at 4.9m reach; Engine Perkins CV12 TCA 1200 26.1 V-12 direct injection 4-stroke diesel.

Between 1988 and 1990 the British Army ordered 80 Challenger ARRV (Rhino) in two batches and the contract was completed with the last vehicles taken into service during 1993. A 50 tank Challenger 1 Regiment has 5 x ARRV, one with each sabre squadron and one with the REME Light Aid Detachment (LAD). This total will probably fall to four in the new 38 tank Challenger 2 Regiment.

The vehicle has a crew of three plus additional space in a separate compartment for another two REME fitters. The vehicle is fitted with two winches (main and auxiliary) plus an Atlas hydraulically operated crane capable of lifting a complete Challenger 2 powerpack. The front dozer blade can be used as a stabiliser blade for the crane or as a simple earth anchor.

Chieftain ARRV are believed to have been withdrawn from service with the RAC.

TRACER

Under current plans, the British Army, RAF Regiment and Royal Marines will be equipped with an entirely new family of light armoured vehicles early in the next century. UK design teams are currently working on a modular/family concept that could replace the range of light armoured vehicles that include Scorpion, Striker, Scimitar, Sultan, Spartan, Sampson, Fox and Ferret.

FFLAV (Future Family of Light Armoured Vehicles) was originally conceived to cover the weight range from approximately 5 to 25 tons, with the majority of the heavier vehicles being tracked and the remainder wheeled. To reduce costs plans were made to use existing, in-production automotive components, many of which could be purchased off the shelf. Such a design policy will almost certainly reduce the cost per vehicle, and make the series attractive in the export market. In addition many vehicles which are currently soft skinned (unarmoured), such as command and communications vehicles, were included in the concept to reduce vulnerability to small arms fire, shell splinters, NBC agents etc.

Following the reduction in the threat, the FFLAV programme has been turned into the LAVS (Light Armoured Vehicle Strategy) which is the programme umbrella for TRACER (Tactical Reconnaissance Armoured Combat Equipment Requirement). TRACER was officially launched in a presentation to industry in September 1992 and the programme will seek to rectify the defects in the CVR(T) Series which were described in the 1992 Statements on the Defence Estimates as follows:-

"The CVR(T) light armoured reconnaissance vehicles were not well suited to fast-moving offensive operations in open country and their employment was constrained by a relative lack of mobility, protection and older generation optics". In June 1993 three consortia were awarded a one-year contract for a feasibility study and report on the TRACER requirement. These three consortia were Royal Ordnance teamed with Alvis, GEC Marconi's Radar and Control Systems teamed with GKN defence and Vickers Defence Systems teamed with Shorts, Siemens Plessey, Teledyne and Texas Instruments. These feasibility studies were completed in April 1994, and following analysis of the studies plus contributions from other MOD Departments, including the Defence Research Agency (DRA), we expect an announcement in 1995 for two of these consortia to be funded to complete a project definition phase followed by a full scale development competition.

We would expect TRACER type vehicles to take on a wide variety of roles, which could include armoured personnel carriers (to replace AFV 432's not included in the Warrior replacement programme) armoured ambulance, communications, reconnaissance, repair and recovery. We also expect there to be a requirement for a simple tank destroyer type vehicle design to mount Trigat LR, and tracked vehicle launch platforms for Rapier 2000. In the initial stages of the project only a basic scout and utility version of the vehicle are planned. It would not be unrealistic to expect to see the first vehicles leave the production line around the year 2005.

We believe that current political developments in Europe, coupled with the reductions in British Forces will reduce the size of this potential TRACER market to approx 750 units (250 reconnaissance and 500 utility) that the only way to achieve volume sales will be within the European Defence Market. Teaming arrangements by major British defence firms such as Alvis, GKN and Vickers will be necessary to penetrate these markets, and there are already reports of European firms such as Krauss Maffei, Thyssen Henschel, Renault, Panard and Oto Melara becoming involved with British manufacturers.

VERDI

VERDI (Vehicle Electronics Research Defence Initiative) is the title for a concept demonstration vehicle in a co-operative programme between the UK MOD, DRA and UK industry. The programme is now at the VERDI II stage where a two man crew operates a modified Warrior using computers, integrated data bases, sensors, weapon systems and electronic displays to fight the vehicle in a closed down, comfortable and ergonomic environment. VERDI gives a glimpse of the armoured vehicle of the future and during a recent exercise a VERDI vehicle was able to sit inside a wood, extend a surveillance mast above the trees and transmit real time images back to a command post via a data link.

We would expect that experience gained in the VERDI programme will have a major impact on the type of vehicle finally adopted in the TRACER programme. The TRACER Reconnaissance vehicle will almost certainly have some resemblance to the VERDI II vehicle.

MARDI

The first MARDI (Mobile Advanced Robotics Defence Initiative) vehicles were involved in field trials during 1993 on Salisbury Plain when a command centre was set up to control an unmanned Streaker vehicle over distances of up to 7 kms. The Streaker vehicle was fitted with a reconnaissance pod containing a TV camera, thermal imager, laser rangefinder and acoustic sensors and can be used for a number of missions including battlefield surveillance, artillery observation and target acquisition.

MARDI also serves as a pointer towards the future, and within twenty years unmanned vehicles datalinked to remote controllers are almost certainly going to be very common on any future battlefield.

MARDI type vehicles will almost certainly be small and fast making them very difficult to locate and destroy. The vehicle design for the World War II Bren Carrier could possibly enjoy a new lease of life.

Sales of Armoured Vehicles

During the 1994-95 Financial Year the UK MOD sold the following armoured vehicles - many at auction to private buyers.

Centurion Armoured Recovery Vehicles	- 54
Humber 1 Ton PIG APC	- 109
Chieftain MBT Mk 10	- 29
Abbot 105mm SP Gun	- 15
Sultan Armoured Command Vehicle	- 17
Fox 30mm Combat Recce Vehicle (wheeled)	- 2
Scorpion 76mm Combat Vehicle Recce (tracked)	- 40
Ferret Scout Car	- 35
Saracen Armoured Personnel Carrier (wheeled)	- 16
AFV 432 APC	- 78
AFV 434 Tracked Engineer Support Vehicle	- 8
M109 155mm SP Guns	- 117

CHAPTER 5 - INFANTRY

"One well known Brigadier always phrases his requirements of the ideal infantryman as 'athlete, stalker, marksman.' I always feel a little inclined to put it on a lower plane and say that the qualities of a successful poacher, cat burglar and gunman would content me".

Field Marshal Lord Wavell (1883-1950)

Regiments and Battalions

The British Infantry is based on the well tried and tested Regimental System; justified regularly on operational deployment, it is based on battalions, which when they number more than one are grouped together to form a "large Regiment". Most Regiments now comprise one Regular and one TA battalion. Regiments are then grouped together within Divisions, which provide a level of administrative command.

The Division of Infantry is an organisation that is responsible for all aspects of military administration, from recruiting, manning and promotions for individuals in the regiments under its wing to the longer term planning required to ensure continuity and cohesion. Divisions of Infantry have no operational command over their regiments, and should not be confused with the operational divisions such as 1(UK) Armd Div and 3(UK) Div.

The Divisions of Infantry are as follows:

The Guards Division	- 5 regular battalions
The Scottish Division	- 6 regular battalions
The Queen's Division	- 6 regular battalions
The King's Division	- 6 regular battalions
The Prince of Wales Division	- 7 regular battalions
The Light Division	- 4 regular battalions

Not administered by Divisions of Infantry but operating under their own administrative arrangements are the following:

The Parachute Regiment	- 3 regular battalions
The Brigade of Gurkhas	- 3 regular battalions
The Royal Irish Regiment	- 1 regular battalion

With the exception of the Guards Division and the Brigade of Gurkhas, all the infantry divisional organisations listed have a varying number of the 36 TA battalions in the British Infantry under their administrative control. In total the British Army will have 41 regular battalions available for service and this total combined with the 36 TA battalions could give a mobilisation strength of 77 infantry battalions (late 1994). Following the announcement of changes in the organisation of the TA, we believe that this total will be reduced and that in the future there will be 29 TA infantry battalions and 4 TA fire support battalions available.

At the beginning of 1995 the infantry was located as follows:

United Kingdom	31 bns (6 Resident in Northern Ireland)
Germany	6 bns
Cyprus	2 bns
Hong Kong	1 bn (Gurkha)
Brunei	1 bn (Gurkha)
Falkland Islands	1 Company Group on detachment
Bosnia	2 bns on detachment

As explained previously it would be most unusual for the Infantry to fight as battalion units especially in armoured or mechanised formations. The HQ of an infantry battalion will generally be the HQ of a battle group, and the force will be provided with armour, artillery and engineers, which will enable it to become a balanced all arms grouping.

Types of Infantry Battalions

Armoured Infantry Battalion - Equipped with Warrior AFV.
Mechanised Infantry Battalion - Equipped with Saxon APC.
Light Role Infantry Battalion - Equipped for General Service.

The other types of battalion are:

Airmobile Infantry Battalion - A battalion with three rifle companies adapted for use with 24 Airmobile Brigade. Total strength is 679 all ranks.

Parachute Battalion - There are three parachute battalions of which two serve with 5 Airborne Brigade at any one time. Total Strength is 679 men.

AMF(L) Battalion - There is one battalion of three rifle companies with an organisation specially tailored for service with the NATO (AMFL). This battalion has 679 men.

Northern Ireland Battalion - This type of infantry battalion has an establishment adapted for long (resident) tours in Northern Ireland. Personnel strength is 644.
Gurkha Infantry Battalion - Equipped for Gurkha requirements.

TA Infantry Battalion - Scaled and equipped to suit the special requirements of the Territorial Army, generally speaking these battalions have three rifle companies.

TA Fire Support Battalion - A new structure with two heavy weapons companies.

Total personnel strength will be 336.

Numbers of Battalions in Specific Roles

a. Infantry Bn (Armd)   - 8
b. Infantry Bn (Mech)   - 4
c. Infantry Bn (Airmob)   - 2
d. Infantry Bn (Light Role)   - 15
e. Infantry Bn (Para)   - 2 (In role)
f. Infantry Bn (NI)   - 6 (Resident in Ulster)
g. Infantry Bn (AMF(L))   - 1
h. Infantry Bn (Gurkha)   - 3
i. Infantry Bn (TA)   - 29
j. Fire Support Bn (TA)   - 4

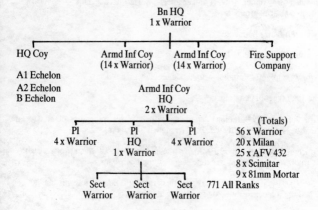

Armoured Infantry Battalion
Commander - Lt Colonel

Bn HQ
1 x Warrior

HQ Coy · Armd Inf Coy (14 x Warrior) · Armd Inf Coy (14 x Warrior) · Fire Support Company

A1 Echelon
A2 Echelon
B Echelon

Armd Inf Coy
HQ
2 x Warrior

Pl — 4 x Warrior · Pl HQ — 1 x Warrior · Pl — 4 x Warrior

Sect Warrior · Sect Warrior · Sect Warrior

(Totals)
56 x Warrior
20 x Milan
25 x AFV 432
8 x Scimitar
9 x 81mm Mortar
771 All Ranks

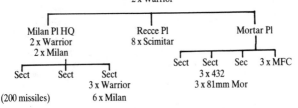

Armoured Infantry Battalion - Fire Support Company
(Commander - Major)
2 x Warrior

Milan Pl HQ
2 x Warrior
2 x Milan

Sect Sect Sect
3 x Warrior
(200 missiles) 6 x Milan

Recce Pl
8 x Scimitar

Mortar Pl

Sect Sect Sec 3 x MFC
3 x 432
3 x 81mm Mor

Note: (1) There are 8 x Armoured Infantry Battalions, 6 of which are in Germany with 1 (UK) Armoured Division and the remaining 2 in the UK with 3 (UK) Division. (2) There are longer term intentions to replace the AFV 432's on issue to armoured infantry battalions by other versions of Warrior or equivalent vehicles such as mortar carrier, ambulance, command vehicle etc.(3) Another 4 Milan firing posts are held by the mobilisation section that is only activated on mobilisation.

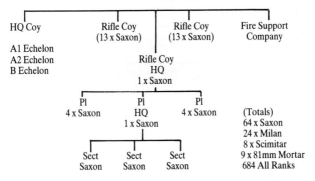

Mechanised Infantry Battalion
(Commander - Lt Colonel)
Bn HQ
3 x Saxon

HQ Coy

A1 Echelon
A2 Echelon
B Echelon

Rifle Coy
(13 x Saxon)

Rifle Coy
HQ
1 x Saxon

Rifle Coy
(13 x Saxon)

Fire Support
Company

Pl
4 x Saxon

Pl
HQ
1 x Saxon

Pl
4 x Saxon

Sect
Saxon

Sect
Saxon

Sect
Saxon

(Totals)
64 x Saxon
24 x Milan
8 x Scimitar
9 x 81mm Mortar
684 All Ranks

Mechanised Infantry Battalion - Fire Support Company
Commander - Major

Milan Pl HQ
2 x Saxon

Recce Pl
8 x Scimitar

Mortar Pl

MG Pl
9 x GPMG(SF)

Sect

Sect
3 x Warrior
6 x Milan

Sect

Mobile
Sect
4 x Milan

Sect

Sect

Sec
3 x 81mm Mor

3 x MFC

Note: (1) In time the Scimitar may be replaced by the new vehicle Sabre (see Chapter 4). This vehicle will be created by taking a Fox turret, mounting it on a Scorpion chassis and replacing the GPMG with a Chain Gun.

Light Role Infantry Battalion
Commander - Lt Colonel

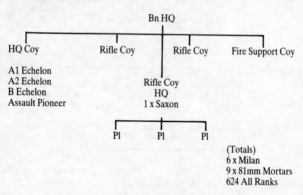

Bn HQ

HQ Coy

Rifle Coy

Rifle Coy

Fire Support Coy

A1 Echelon
A2 Echelon
B Echelon
Assault Pioneer

Rifle Coy
HQ
1 x Saxon

Pl

Pl

Pl

(Totals)
6 x Milan
9 x 81mm Mortars
624 All Ranks

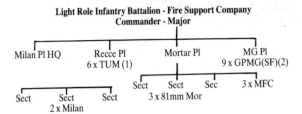

Light Role Infantry Battalion - Fire Support Company
Commander - Major

Milan Pl HQ — Recce Pl (6 x TUM (1)) — Mortar Pl — MG Pl (9 x GPMG(SF)(2))

Sect — Sect — Sect (2 x Milan)

Sect — Sect — Sec (3 x 81mm Mor) — 3 x MFC

Notes: (1) TUM is the abbreviation for Truck-Utility-Medium; (2) General Purpose Machine Guns mounted on tripods with a range of up to 1,800 metres.

Territorial Army Infantry Battalion

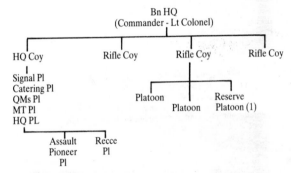

Bn HQ
(Commander - Lt Colonel)

HQ Coy — Rifle Coy — Rifle Coy — Rifle Coy

Signal Pl
Catering Pl
QMs Pl
MT Pl
HQ PL

Assault Pioneer Pl — Recce Pl

Platoon — Platoon — Reserve Platoon (1)

Notes: (1) On mobilisation the reserve platoon would be activated and manned by reservists. (2) TA battalions with a role in support of the ARRC have Milan and Mortar Platoons attached from the TA Fire Support Battalion as necessary. (3) Expect a TA battalion with a National Defence Role to have approximately 600 men on mobilisation and a battalion with a role in support of the ARRC to have approximately 700.

Territorial Army Fire Support Battalion

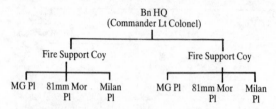

Total strength of this new type of TA battalion will be in the region of approximately 370 personnel. The following TA battalions are being converted to this new role:

> 3rd Bn The Prince of Wales's Own Regiment of Yorkshire
> 3rd Bn The Cheshire Regiment
> 5th Bn The Royal Green Jackets
> 51st Highland Volunteers

It is believed that these fire support battalions will start training for their new role in April 1995 with a first support weapons concentration in 1996. Current plans suggest that these battalions could be operational by 1 April 1997. There has been considerable speculation regarding the role of the 5th Bn The Royal Green Jackets who may in the longer term be invited to train one of their companies in the parachute role.

The Special Air Service

The SAS (Special Air Service) can be considered as part of the Infantry and the single regular Regiment is designed for special operations. SAS soldiers are selected from other branches of the Army after exhaustive selection tests. There are two battalions of TA SAS.

Platoon Organisation

The basic building bricks of the Infantry Battalion are the platoon and the section. Under normal circurstances expect a British infantry platoon to resemble the organisation in the following diagram:

Armoured or Mechanised Infantry Platoon

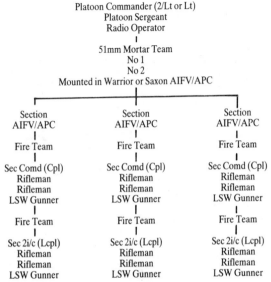

Platoon Commander (2/Lt or Lt)
Platoon Sergeant
Radio Operator

51mm Mortar Team
No 1
No 2
Mounted in Warrior or Saxon AIFV/APC

Section AIFV/APC	Section AIFV/APC	Section AIFV/APC
Fire Team	Fire Team	Fire Team
Sec Comd (Cpl)	Sec Comd (Cpl)	Sec Comd (Cpl)
Rifleman	Rifleman	Rifleman
Rifleman	Rifleman	Rifleman
LSW Gunner	LSW Gunner	LSW Gunner
Fire Team	Fire Team	Fire Team
Sec 2i/c (Lcpl)	Sec 2i/c (Lcpl)	Sec 2i/c (Lcpl)
Rifleman	Rifleman	Rifleman
Rifleman	Rifleman	Rifleman
LSW Gunner	LSW Gunner	LSW Gunner

Notes:

(1) The platoon could be reinforced by a two man team armed with the GPMG in the Sustained Fire (SF) Role. In most regular battalions the GPMG SF gunners are concentrated in the Fire Support Company.

(2) The whole platoon with the exception of the LSW (Light Support Weapon) gunners are armed with IW - SA80 (Individual Weapon).

(3) The APC could be either Warrior or Saxon and possibly AFV 432.

(4) Platoons in armoured or mechanised infantry battalions are armed with the LAW 80 for anti-tank operations.

The Royal Irish Regiment

The Royal Irish Regiment was formed in July 1992 following the merger of the Ulster Defence Regiment and the Royal Irish Rangers. The Royal Irish Regiment is comprised of 1 x General Service and 6 x Home Service Battalions.

The General Service Battalion operates as does any other unit of the Army. The Home Service battalions serve only in Northern Ireland except for occasional training overseas and include both full time and part time soldiers. The overall strength of the Royal Irish Regiment is about 5,600 men and women.

Royal Irish Regiment (Home Service) Strength (1 April 1993)

Males	2,627	(Full Time)	
Females	290	(Full Time)	
Males	2,341	(Part Time)	
Females	355	(Part Time)	
Total	5,613		

The Royal Irish Regiment currently has seven battalions:

General Service   -   1 R Irish

Home Service   -   3 R Irish (Co Down & Co Armagh)
4 R Irish (Co Fermanagh & Co Tyrone)
5 R Irish (Co Londonderry)
7 R Irish (City of Belfast)
8 R Irish (Co Tyrone)
9 R Irish (Co Antrim)

AFV 432

(Approx 2,000 in service): Crew 2 (Commander and Driver): Weight loaded 15,280kg: Length 5.25m: Width 2.8m: Height 2.28m: Ground Pressure 0.78kg km squared: Armament 1 x 7.62 Machine Gun; 2 x 3 barrel smoke dischargers: Engine Rolls Royce K60 No.4 Mark 1-4: Engine Power 240bhp: Fuel Capacity 454 litres: Max Road Speed 52kph: Road Range 580km: Vertical Obstacle 0.9m: Trench Crossing 2.05m: Gradient 60 degrees: Carries up to 10 men : Armour 12.7mm max.

In the medium term the AFV 432 (Trojan) will continue to provide the majority of the British Army's armoured vehicle fleet and it will be some considerable time before all the vehicles in service are replaced. First produced in 1962 and following a development line going back to WWII, the AFV 432 has been produced in 4 marks, capable of fulfilling about 14 different roles. The most important of these roles are, Command Post APC, 81mm Mor Carrier, Ambulance, Artillery Observation Post, Field Artillery Computing Equipment (FACE) Carrier, Minelayer, Cymbeline Radar Carrier and basic Infantry Troop Carrier.

The vehicle is NBC proof and when necessary can be converted for swimming when it has a water speed of 6kph. Properly maintained it is a rugged and reliable vehicle with a good cross country performance. The most serious drawback is the lack of vision ports for all less the crew and their subsequent disorientation after dismounting.

MCV - 80 Fv 510 (Warrior)

(On order 789 - and approximately 750 believed to be in service at the beginning of 1995). Weight loaded 24,500kg: Length 6.34m: Height to turret top 2.78m: Width 3.0m: Ground Clearance 0.5m: Max Road Speed 75kph: Road Range 500km: Engine Rolls Royce CV8 diesel: Horsepower 550hp: Crew 2 (carries 8 infantry soldiers): Armament L21 30mm Rarden Cannon: Coaxial EX-34 7.62mm Chain Gun: Smoke Dischargers Royal Ordnance Visual and Infra Red Screening Smoke (VIRSS).

Warrior is an armoured infantry fighting vehicle (AIFV) that replaced the AFV 432 in the armoured infantry battalions. Following drawdown the original buy of 1,048 vehicles was reduced and in early 1993 it was announced that the total buy had been reduced to 789 units. The vehicle is in service with 2 armoured infantry battalions in the UK (with 3 (UK) Div) and 6 armoured infantry battalions in Germany (with 1 (UK) Armd Div). Warrior armed with the 30mmm Rarden cannon gives the crew a good chance of destroying enemy APC's at ranges of up to 1,500m and the vehicle carries an infantry section of seven men.

The vehicle is NBC proof, and a full range of night vision equipment is included as standard. The basic Warrior is part of a family of vehicles which include a milan carrier, a mechanised recovery vehicle, an engineer combat version and an artillery command vehicle to name but a few. Examination of the contract details reveal that each vehicle will cost approximately £550,000.

The vehicle has seen successful operational service in the Gulf (1991) and with the British contingent serving with the UN in Bosnia. Warrior has proven protection against mines, and there is dramatic BBC TV footage of a Warrior running over a Serbian anti-tank mine with little or no serious damage to the vehicle.

The Kuwait MOD has signed a contract for the purchase of Warrior vehicles some of which are Recce vehicles armed with a 90mm Cockerill gun. Industry sources suggest that the Kuwait contract is for 230 vehicles.

AFV 103 Spartan

(400 in service). Crew 3: Weight 8,172kg: Length 5.12m: Height 2.26m: Width 2.26m: Ground Clearance 0.35m: Max Road Speed 80kph: Road Range 483kms: Engine Jaguar J60 No.1 Mark 100B: Engine Power 190bhp: Fuel Capacity 386 litres: Ammunition Carried 3,000 rounds of 7.62mm: Armament 1 x 7.62 Machine Gun.

Spartan is the APC of the Combat Vehicle Reconnaissance Tracked (CVRT) series of vehicles, which includes, Fv 102 Striker, Fv 104 Samaritan, Fv 105 Sultan, Fv 106 Sampson and Fv 107 Scimitar. Spartan is a very small APC that can only carry 4 men in addition to the crew of 3. It is therefore used to carry small specialised groups such as the reconnaissance teams, air defence sections, mortar fire controllers and ambush parties.
Samaritan, Sultan and Sampson are also APC type vehicles, Samaritan is the CVRT ambulance vehicle, Sultan is the armoured command vehicle and Sampson is an armoured recovery vehicle.

Spartan is in service with the following nations: Belgium - 266:
Oman - 6 Philippines - 7.

AT - 105 Saxon

(664 in service-) Weight 10,670kg: Length 5.16m: Width 2.48m: Height 2.63m: Ground Clearance (axles) 0.33m: Max Road Speed 96kph: Max Road Range 510km: Fuel Capacity 160 litres: Fording 1.12m: Gradient 60 degrees: Engine Bedford 600 6-cylinder diesel developing 164bhp at 2,800rpm: Armour proof against 7.62 rounds fired at point blank range: Crew 2 + 10 max.

The Saxon is manufactured by GKN Defence and the first of the 664 units for the British Army were delivered in late 1983. The vehicle, which can be best described as a battlefield taxi is designed around truck parts and does not require the enormous maintenance of track and running gear normally associated with APC/AIFVs. Capable of travelling across very rough terrain and fording over 3' of water, the Saxon is a welcome addition to the inventory of infantry units in UKLF providing much needed battlefield mobility. The vehicle is fitted with a 7.62mm Machine Gun for LLAD.

Each vehicle costs over £100,000 at 1984 prices and they are on issue to 4 mechanised infantry battalions assigned to 3 (UK) Division. The vehicle has been used very sucessfully by British mechanised battalions serving with the UN in Bosnia where the addition of an L37 turret has enhanced its firepower.

Saxon is in service with the following overseas customers: Bahrain - 10: Brunei - 24: Hong Kong - 6: Malaysia - 40: Oman - 15.

During 1993 the British Army took delivery of the Saxon patrol vehicle for service in Northern Ireland. This new vehicle has a Cummins BT 5.1 engine instead of the Beford 6 cyclinder installed on the APC version and other enhancements for internal security operations such as roof mounted searchlights, improved armour, a barricade removal device and an anti-wire device.

Saxon Patrol comes in two versions, troop carrier and ambulance. The troop carrier carries ten men and the ambulance 2 stretcher cases. Industry sources suggest that this latest contract was for 137 vehicles at a cost of some £20 million resulting in a unit cost per vehicle of approximately £145,000.

Shorland

Weight loaded 3,360kg: Length 4.59m: Height 2.28m: Weight 1.77m: Max Road Speed 88kph: Engine Rover 6-cylinder: Fuel Capacity of 64 litres: Armament 30 Browning or 7.62 machine guns.

Based on the Land Rover chassis, Short Brothers of Belfast produced a lightly armoured vehicle for patrolling in Ulster which is in service with the Royal Ulster Constabulary, and the Royal Irish Regiment.

Milan 2

Missile - Max Range 2,000m; Min Range 25m; Length 918mm; Weight 6.73Kg; Diameter 125mm; Wing Span 267mm; Rate of Fire 3-4rpm; Warhead - Weight 2.70kg; Diameter 115mm; Explosive Content 1.79kg;
Firing Post- Weight 16.4kg; Length 900mm; Height 650mm; Width 420mm; Armour Penetration 352mm; Time of Flight to Max Range 12.5 secs; Missile Speed 720kph; Guidance Semi-Automatic command to line of sight by means of wires:

Milan is a second generation anti-tank weapon, the result of a joint development project between France and West Germany with British Milan launchers and missiles built under licence in the UK by British Aerospace Dynamics. We believe that the cost of a Milan missile is currently in the region of £9,000 and that to date the UK MOD has purchased over 50,000 missiles.

The Milan comes in two main components which are the launcher and the missile, it then being a simple matter to clip both items together and prepare the system for use. On firing the operator has only to keep his aiming mark on the target and the SACLOS guidance system will do the rest.

Milan was the first of a series of infantry anti-tank weapons that seriously started to challenge the supremacy of the main battle tank on the battlefield. During fighting in Chad in 1987 it appears that 12 Chadian Milan post mounted on Toyota Light Trucks were able to account for over 60 Libyan T-55's and T-62's. Reports from other conflicts suggest similar results.

Milan is on issue throughout the British Army and an armoured infantry battalion could be expected to be equipped with 24 firing posts and 200 missiles. In the longer term we expect to see Milan replaced by Trigat MR in the latter part of the decade. Milan is in service with 36 nations world-wide and it is believed that over 1,000 firing posts are in service with the British Army.

Trigat MR

Range 2000m: Missile Weight 16kg: Firing Post Weight 20kg.

Trigat MR (Medium Range) is a manportable or vehicle borne, third generation anti-tank missile system designed to replace Milan in service with the British Army. Trigat MR is a medium range missile (2000m) with SACLOS beam riding guidance. Launch will be low velocity, with thrust vectoring keeping the missile airborne as the aerodynamic surfaces come into effect.

The missile is the result of a European collaborative project with the three main partners being France, Germany and the UK. The manufacturer is Euromissile Dynamics Group (EDMG). Current predictions are that the missiles may cost as much as £25,000 each by the time that the system is accepted into service. We believe that Trigat MR should appear in service during December 1998.

LAW 80

Effective Range Up to 500m: Armour Penetration Up to 650mm: Impact Sensor - Scrub and Foliage Proof: Launcher Length (Firing Mode) 1.5m: Launcher Length (Carrying Mode) 1m: Carrying Weight 10kg: Projectile Diameter 94mm: Temperature Range -46 to +65 degrees C: Rear Danger Area 20m.

LAW 80 has replaced the 84mm Carl Gustav and the US 66mm in service with the British Army, and infantry units in armoured and mechanised battalions are equipped down to section level with this weapon. The latest materials and explosives technology have been utilised in this one-man portable weapon which is capable of destroying main battle tanks at ranges of up to 500m. Outstanding accuracy against both static and moving targets is achieved by the use of a built-in semi-automatic spotting rifle which reduces aiming errors prior to firing the main projectile. This feature roughly doubles the first-shot kill probability and the shaped charge warhead penetrates armour in excess of 650mm. In addition to the low light performance of the built in sight, full night capability is available using a night sight.

Hunting Engineering has also developed a range of systems to fire the weapon remotely.

Each system utilises a standard LAW 80 with identical tripod and firing unit. ADDERMINE - is suitable as an off-route mine and is fired when a trip or break wire is disturbed. ADDERMINE/ARGES- is a fully autonomous off-route mine system. The programmable sensor package is capable of selecting a particular target before firing. ADDERLAZE - provides the remote capability to engage single or multiple targets at ranges of up to 2kms by the use of a coded laser pulse to fire the weapon.

81mm L16 Mortar

(500 in service) Max Range HE 5,650m: Elevation 45 degrees to 80 degrees: Muzzle Velocity 255m/s: Length of barrel 1280mm: Weight of barrel 12.7kg: Weight of base plate 11.6kg: In action Weight 35.3kg: Bomb Weight HE L3682 4.2kg: Rate of Fire 15rpm: Calibre 81mm.

The 81mm Mortar is on issue to all infantry battalions (with the exception of General Service TA battalions), with each battalion having a mortar platoon with 3 sections; and each section deploying 3 mortars. These mortars are the battalions organic fire support and can be used to put a very heavy weight of fire down on an objective in an extremely short period. Mortar fire is particularly lethal to infantry in the open and in addition is very useful for neutralising dug in strongpoints or forcing armour to close down.

The fire of each mortar section is controlled by the MFC (Mortar Fire Controller) who is usually an NCO and generally positioned well forward with the troops being supported. Most MFCs will find themselves either very close to or co-located with a company commander. The MFC informs the base plate (mortar position) by radio of the location of the target and then corrects the fall of the bombs, directing them onto the target.

Mortar fire can be used to suppress enemy positions until assaulting troops arrive within 200-300m of the position. The mortar fire then lifts onto enemy counter attack and supporting positions while the assault goes in. The 81mm Mortar can also assist with smoke and illuminating rounds.

The mortar is carried in and fired from an AFV432 or a converted Land Rover and if necessary can be carried in two man portable 11.35kg loads and one 12.28kg load. In the past, infantry companies have carried one 81mm round per man when operating in areas such as Borneo where wheeled or tracked transport was not available.

Trials are currently being conducted using the BAe 81mm Merlin Anti Tank round that uses a millimetric seeker to identify stationary and moving armoured targets over a footprint area of 300m x 300m. The seeker relays information to the guidance system that then guides the mortar round onto the target.

51mm Light Mortar

(2093 in service) Range 750m: Bomb Weight 800gms (illum), 900gms (smk), 920gms (HE): Rapid Rate of Fire 8rpm: Length of barrel 750mm: Weight Complete 6.275kg: Calibre 51.25mm

The 51mm Light Mortar is a weapon that can be carried and fired by one man, and is found in the HQ of an infantry platoon. The mortar is used to fire smoke, illuminating and HE rounds out to a range of approximately 750m; a short range insert device enables the weapon to be used in close quarter battle situations with some accuracy. The 51mm Light Mortar has replaced the older l940s 2" mortar.

5.56mm Individual Weapon (IW) (SA 80)

Effective Range 400m: Muzzle Velocity 940m/s: Rate of Fire from 610-775rpm: Weight 4.98kg (with 30 round magazine): Length Overall 785mm: Barrel Length 518mm: Trigger Pull 3.12-4.5kg:

Designed to fire the standard NATO 5.56mm x 45mm round the SA 80 is fitted with an X4 telescopic (SUSAT) sight as standard. Although some modification work is still in progress, the vast majority of the British Army is now equipped with this weapon. The total buy for SA 80 is for 332,092 weapons. Issues of the weapon are believed to be as follows:

Royal Navy	7,864
Royal Marines	8,350
Royal Air Force	42,221
MOD Police	1878
Army	271,779

At 1991/92 prices the total cost of the SA80 Contract was in the order of £384.16 million. By late 1994 some 10,000 SA 80 Night Sights and 3rd Generation Image Intensifier Tubes had been delivered almost completing the contract.

Prior to the entry of the weapon into general service, during 1983 the Infantry Trials and Development Unit (ITDU) at Warminster in Wiltshire conducted comparitive tests on both the SA80 and the SLR using the old SLR APWT (Annual Personal Weapons Test) for both weapons. The results were as follows:

Results	SLR	SA80 with SUSAT
Passes	72%	100%
Marksmanship Standard	17%	51%
Average Score	53	60

Note: The highest possible score was 70; the pass mark 49 and the marksmanship standard was 60 out of a possible 70. The Army Small Arms Shooting Policy has since been amended to take into account the greater accuracy of the SA 80.

The weapon has had a mixed press and much has been made of the 32 modifications that have been made to the SA80 since 1983. Although there are many critics outside of the services, in the main the serving soldiers that we have spoken to have praised the weapon, and those that have had experience on both the SLR and SA80 are unstinting in their praise for the newer system.

The bottom line is probably that the SA80 is a highly accurate weapon and one that is more than sound when properly maintained. It's accuracy places it into a different generation from earlier weapons and it needs to be treated with respect for its higher technology. Our own enquiries suggest that it compares favourably with anything else available on the current world market.

5.56mm Light Support Weapon (LSW)

Range 1,000m: Muzzle Velocity 970m/s: Length 900mm: Barrel Length 646mm: Weight Loaded with 30 round magazine 6.58kg: Rate of Fire from to 610-775rpm.

The LSW has been developed to replace the GPMG in the light role and about 80% of the parts are interchangeable with the 5.56 IW (SA 80). A great advantage for the infantryman is the ability of both weapons to take the same magazines. A rifle section will have two x 4 man fire teams and each fire team 1 x LSW.

7.62mm Self Loading Rifle (SLR)

Effective Range 600m: Muzzle Velocity 838m/s: Rate of Fire (Rapid) 20rpm: Weight 5.07kg (with 20 round magazine): Length Overall 1.43m.

The standard rifle of the British Army until the late 1980s, this weapon has been in service since the mid 1950s and has been replaced by the SA 80. There could be some examples of this weapon around until the latter part of the decade.

7.62mm General Purpose Machine Gun (GPMG)

Range 800 (Light Role), 1,800m (Sustained Fire Role): Muzzle Velocity 538m/s: Length 1.23m: Weight loaded 13.85kg (gun + 50 rounds): Belt Fed: Rate of Fire up to 750rpm: Rate of Fire Light Role 100rpm: Rate of Fire Sustained Fire Role 200rpm.

The Standard infantry machine gun which has been in service since the early 1960s, the GPMG can be used in the light role fired from a bipod or can be fitted to a tripod for use in the sustained fire role. The gun is also found pintle mounted on many armoured vehicles. Used on a tripod the gun is effective out to 1,800m although it is difficult to spot strike at this range because the tracer rounds in the ammunition belt burns out at 1,100m. The GPMG has been replaced in the light role by the 5.56mm Light Support Weapon (LSW). The LSW weighs approximately half as much as the GPMG. Machine Gun platoons in infantry battalions remain equipped with the GPMG in the sustained fire role.

CHAPTER 6 - ARTILLERY

"The history of artillery is the history of progress in the sciences, and is therefore the history of civilisation."

Charles Bonaparte (Napoleon III) 1808-73

"There can never be too many guns, there are never enough of them".

Ferdinand Foch 1851-1929

The Royal Regiment of Artillery (RA)

The RA provides the battlefield fire support and air defence for the British Army in the field. Its various regiments are equipped for conventional fire support using field guns, for area and point air defence using air defence missiles and for specialised artillery locating tasks. By September 1990 the first Regiment equipped with the Multiple Launch Rocket System (MLRS) had taken its place in the Order of Battle and these weapons were used with great effect during the war in the Gulf.

By early 1995 the RA, one of the larger organisations in the British Army with 17 Regiments included in its Order of Battle, will have the following structure in both the UK and Germany (ARRC).

	UK	Germany
Field Regiments (AS 90 SP Guns)	2	3
Field Regiments (FH70 or Light Gun)	3(1)	-
Depth Fire Regiments (MLRS)	2	1
Air Defence Regiments (Rapier)	2	1
Air Defence Regiment (Javelin)	1	
Air Defence Regiment (HVM)	-	1
Training Regiment	1	-
The Kings Troop (Ceremonial)	1	-

Note: (1) Of these 3 Reiments 1 is a Commando Regiment (29 Cdo Regt) and another a Parachute Regiment (7 RHA). (2) Although the artillery is organised into Regiments, much of a "gunner's" loyalty is directed towards the battery in which he serves. A Regiment will generally have three or four batterys under command. Following "Options for Change" by late 1994 the Artillery will have reduced from 23 Regiments (76 titled batterys) to 17 Regiments (56 titled batterys).

The Royal Horse Artillery (RHA) is also part of the Royal Regiment of Artillery and its three regiments have been included in the totals above.
There is considerable cross posting of officers and soldiers from the RA to the RHA, and some consider service with the RHA to be a career advancement.

Artillery training is carried out at the Royal School of Artillery at Larkhill in Wiltshire. After initial training officers and gunners will be posted to RA units world-wide, but soldiers will return to the RSA for frequent career and employment courses. Artillery recruits spend the first period of recruit training (Common Military Syllabus) at the Army Training Regiment - Litchfield.

The equipment available to artillery is changing fast and the computerised locating and fire control systems now coming into service, combined with "intelligent" munitions and long range weapon platforms threaten to create another revolution in tactical thinking. This revolution may have the same effect on land warfare as the emergence of the tank.

A new generation of Rocket Launchers (MLRS) and Self Propelled Field Guns (AS 90), with very long ranges and ordnance with devastating terminal effect is now appearing on the battlefield. These weapons, fearsome though they may be, are all the more destructive when linked to modern target location systems. These locating systems, such as small, fast and highly manoeuvrable remotely piloted vehicles are capable of flying out over enemy territory, sending back real time up to the minute TI (thermal imagery) pictures of the target area and assisting observers in directing the rounds onto the target.

Artillery has always been a cost effective way of destroying or neutralising targets. When the cost of a battery of guns, (approx £8 million) is compared with the cost of a close air support aircraft, (£16 million) and the cost of training each pilot, (£3 million +) the way ahead for governments with less and less to spend on defence is clear.

Air Defence is a vital part of the role of the Royal Artillery and updates to the Rapier system continue, with batterys being upgraded to Field Standard B2 and Field Standard C. During 1994 a Starstreak HVM Regiment became operational in the UK. In addition, the air defences will be enhanced by the Air Defence Alerting Device for Javelin and Starstreak, and the Air Defence Command, Control and Information System entered service during late 1994.

The Royal Artillery provides the modern British armoured formation with a protective covering. The air defence covers the immediate airspace above and around the formation, with the field artillery reaching out to approximately 30kms in front and across the flanks of the formation. An armoured formation that moves out of this protective covering is open to immediate destruction by an intelligent enemy as the Egyptians discovered in 1973.

Divisional Artillery Group (DAG)

An armoured or mechanised division has it own artillery under command. This artillery usually consists of 3 Close Support Regiments, with a number of units detached from the Corps Artillery and could include TA reinforcements from the UK. In war the composition of the DAG will vary from division to division according to the task.

Armoured Divisional Artillery Group (DAG)

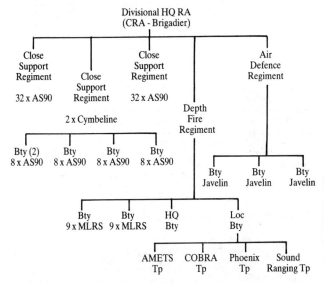

(Notes:)
(1) This is a diagram of the artillery support available to 1(UK) Armd Div deployed with the ARRC in Germany. Expect each brigade in the division to have one Close Support Regiment with AS90 under command.

(2) The number of batterys and final number of guns per battery in an AS90 Close Support Regiment appears to have been finally resolved at 4 batterys of eight guns per battery, to enable the 4 battlegroups in each brigade to be fully supported. Although a battery has eight guns on establishment only six guns will be manned in peacetime.

(3) Air defended areas (ADAs) are provided by Rapier. There is one Rapier Regiment in Germany and one in the UK.

(4) Expect all AS90 deliveries to be complete during 1996.

(5) The Staff of an armoured or mechanised division includes a Brigadier of Artillery known as the Commander Royal Artillery (CRA). The CRA acts as the artillery advisor to the Divisional Commander, and would probably assign one of his Close Support Regiments to support each of the Brigades in the division. These regiments would be situated in positions that would allow most of their batterys to fire across the complete divisional front. Therefore, in the very best case, a battlegroup under extreme threat could be supported by the fire of more than 96 guns.

Artillery Fire Support

A square brigade (of two infantry battalions and 2 armoured regiments) will probably have a Close Support Regiment of 4 Batterys in support, and the CO of this regiment will act as the artillery adviser to the Brigade Commander.
It would be usual to expect that each of the 4 battlegroups in the brigade would have a Battery Commander acting as the artillery advisor to the Battlegroup Commander. The 3 Combat Teams or Squadron/Company Groups in the Battlegroup would each be provided with a Forward Observation Officer (FOO), who is responsible for directing the fire of the guns onto the target.
The FOO and his party travel in armoured vehicles to enable them to keep up with the formation being supported and there is a specialised FOO Warrior variant in production.

The FOO is in direct communication with:

(a) The Gun Position
(b) The Battery Commander at BGHQ
(c) The Regimental Fire Direction Centre.

Having identified the target, the FOO will call for fire from the guns, and he will then adjust the fall of shot to cover the target area. The FOO will be assisted in this task by the use of a Warrior OP vehicle containing the computerised fire control equipment which provides accurate data of the target location.

Given a vehicle with its surveillance and target acquisition suite the FOO can almost instantly obtain the correct grid of the target and (the Gunners claim) without calling for corrections, order 1 round fire for effect.

M109 A2

(Some 50 remain in service). Crew 6: Weight loaded 23,796kg: Length 6.09m: Height 3.04m: Width 3.14m: Max Road Speed 55kph: Road Range 120km: Engine one 405 - hp Detroit Diesel Model 8V71T turbo-charged in-line diesel: Ammo Capacity 28 rounds of HE, Smoke; Illuminating; Canister, Chemical or Nuclear ammunition; Calibre 155mm: Muzzle Velocity 684m/s: Shell Weight (HE) 43kg: Maximum Range (HE) 18kms: Armour 38mm max: Rapid Rate of Fire 3rpm.

The M109 A1 is the SP gun that is currently deployed with some of the present Close Support Regiments of 1 (UK) Armoured Division in Germany.
The 155mm round is a far more powerful munition than that of the 105mm Abbot and is far more effective against all types of target.

A US weapon which first saw service in the early 1960s, it is believed that the M109s in British service do not fire either nuclear or chemical rounds.
It would appear that the M109s will stay in service long enough to fill the gap between the first deliveries of AS90 and the end of the production run. We therefore see the last of these guns being retired from service at some time during 1995.

There are currently 7,303 M109 in service with 28 nations, the vast majority (2,400) being in service with the United States Army and Marines.

(AS 90)
(179 on order) Crew 5: Length 9.07m: Width 3.3m: Height 3.0m overall: Ground Clearance 0.41m: Turret Ring Diameter 2.7m: Armour 17mm: Calibre 155mm: Range (39 cal) 24.7kms (52 cal) 30kms: Recoil Length 780mm: Rate of Fire 3 rounds in 10 secs (burst) 6 rounds per minute (intense) 2 rounds per minute (sustained): Secondary Armament 7.62mm MG: Traverse 6,400 mills: Elevation -89/+1.244 mills: Ammunition Carried 48 x 155mm projectiles and charges (31 turret & 17 hull): Engine Cummins VTA903T turbo-charged V8 diesel 660hp: Max Speed 53 kph: Gradient 60%: Vertical Obstacle 0.75m: Trench Crossing 2.8m: Fording Depth 1.5m: Road Range 420kms.

AS 90 is manufactured by Vickers Shipbuilding and Engineering (VSEL) at Barrow in Furness and has recently been the subject of an order for 179 guns under a fixed price contract for £300 million. These 179 guns will equip 5 field regiments completely replacing the Abbot and M109 in British service. The first Regiment to receive AS 90 was 1st Regiment Royal Horse Artillery (1 RHA) in October 1993, followed by issues to 3 RHA, 4 Regt, 40 Regt and 26 Regt. Each Regiment will receive 4 batterys of eight guns, of which six will be manned in peacetime. Three of these Regiments will be under the command of 1(UK) Armoured Division in Germany and two under the command of 3 (UK) Div in the United Kingdom. Production is scheduled to reach three per week from May 1993 and production of AS 90 should be complete by late 1995.

AS 90 is currently equipped with a 39 calibre gun which fires the NATO L15 unassisted projectile out to a range of 24.7kms (RAP range is 30kms). It is believed that future production models may have the 52 calibre gun with ranges of 30kms (unassisted) and 40kms (assisted projectile). Indications are that the current in service date for the 52 calibre gun is 1998.

AS 90 has been fitted with an autonomous navigation and gun laying system (AGLS), enabling it to work independently of external sighting references. Central to the system is is an inertial dynamic reference unit (DRU) taken from the US Army's MAPS (Modular Azimuth Positioning System). The bulk of the turret electronics are housed in the Turret Control Computer (TCC) which controls the main turret functions, including gunlaying, magazine control, loading systems control, power distribution and testing.

VSEL have major plans for the sale of this system and believe that there is a potential world market for over 1,000 units.

227mm MLRS

(62 launchers in service - 54 operational in 3 Regiments): Crew 3: Weight loaded 24,756kg: Weight Unloaded 19,573kg: Length 7.167m: Width 2.97m: Height (stowed) 2.57m: Height (max elevatation) 5.92m: Ground Clearance 0.43m: Max Road Speed 64kph: Road Range 480km: Fuel Capacity 617 litres: Fording 1.02m: Vertical Obstacle 0.76m: Engine Cummings VTA-903 turbo-charged 8 cylinder diesel developing 500 bhp at 2,300 rpm: Rocket Diameter 227mm: Rocket Length 3.93m: M77 Bomblet Rocket Weight 302.5kg: AT2 SCATMIN Rocket Weight 254.46kg: M77 Bomblet Range 11.5 -32kms: AT2 SCATMIN Rocket Range 39kms: One round "Fire for Effect" equals one launcher firing 12 rockets: Ammunition Carried 12 rounds (ready to fire).

The British Army has purchased MLRS to replace the M107 SP Guns that were previously deployed with Corps Artillery Heavy Regiments. The MLRS is based on the US M2 Bradley chassis and the system is self loaded with 2 x rocket pod containers, each containing 6 x rockets. The whole loading sequence is power assisted and loading takes between 20 and 40 minutes. There is no manual proceedure.

A single round "Fire for Effect" (12 rockets) delivers 7728 bomblets or 336 scatterable mines and the coverage achieved is considered sufficient to neutalise a 500m x 500m target or produce a minefield of a similar size. The weapon system is range dependent and therefore more rounds will be required to guarantee the effect as the range to the target increases. Ammunition for the MLRS is carried on the DROPS vehicle which is a Medium Mobility Load Carrier. Each DROPS vehicle with a trailer can carry 8 x Rocket Pod Containers and there are 15 x DROPS vehicles supporting the 9 x M270 Launcher vehicles within each MLRS battery.

The handling of MLRS is almost a military "art form" and is an excellent example of the dependence of modern artillery on high technology. Getting the best out of the system is more than just parking the tubes and firing in the direction of the enemy. MLRS is the final link in a chain that includes almost everything available on the modern battlefield, from high speed communications, collation of intelligence, logistics and a multitude of high technology artillery skills and drills. Remotely piloted vehicles can be used to acquire targets, real time TV and data links are used to move information from target areas to formation commanders and onward to the firing positions. Helicopters can be used to dump ammunition and in some cases to move firing platforms.

MLRS will probably be deployed as independent launcher units, using "shoot-and-scoot" techniques. A battery of nine launchers will be given a battery manoeuvre area (BMA), within which are allocated three troop manoeuvre areas (TMA). These TMAs will contain close hides, survey points and reload points. In a typical engagement, a single launcher will be given its fire mission orders using burst data transmission.

An important initial piece of information received is the "drive on angle"; the crew will drive the launcher out of the hide (usually less than 100m) and align it with this angle. Using the navigation equipment, its location is fed into the ballistic computer which already has the full fire mission details. The launcher is then elevated and fired and the process can take as little as a few minutes to complete.

As soon as conditions allow, the vehicle will leave the firing location and go to a reload point where it will unload the empty rocket pods and pick up full ones; this can be done in less than five minutes. It will then go to a new hide within the TMA via a survey point to check the accuracy of the navigation system (upon which the accuracy of fire is entirely dependent). The whole of this cycle is coordinated centrally, and details of the new hide and reload point are received as part of the fire mission orders. The complete cycle from firing to being in a new hide ready for action might take half an hour.

In a typical day, a battery could move once or twice to a new BMA but this could impose a strain upon the re-supply system unless well planned (bearing in mind the need for the ammunition to be in position before the launcher vehicle arrives in a new BMA).

The frequent moves are a result of security problems inherent in MLRS's use. In addition to attack by radar-controlled counterbattery fire, its effectiveness as an interdiction weapon makes it a valuable target for special-forces units. Although MLRS will be hidden amongst friendly forces up to 15km behind the FEBA, its firing signature and small crew (three) will force it to move continually to avoid an actual confrontation with enemy troops.

The US Army is currently operating 416 MLRS and by the middle of the decade the French will have 82, the West Germans 206 and the Italians 21.

FH-70 Howitzer

(72 in service). Crew 8: Weight (in firing position) 8,800kg: Length 9.45m: Height 2.56m: Ammunition HE, AT, Smoke, Illuminating: Maximum Range HE 24kms: Calibre 155mm: Rate of Fire 6rpm: Shell Weight (HE) 43.5kg: Engine Volkswagen 1,795cc petrol producing 76bhp with a 20km range.

The FH-70 is the result of a NATO collaborative project between Italy, West Germany and the United Kingdom. The first FH-70 were delivered to the British Army in 1978 and there are now 79 guns in service. Recent "Options for Change" restructuring has seen the withdrawal of the FH-70 from all but one regular field regiment and the gun is now in service with both 100 and 101 Regiments of the Territorial Army.

The gun is designed to enable NATO forces to use the 155mm round which is capable of disrupting massed armoured formations. The gun is towed into action by the FH 70 Foden, 6 x 6 Tractor and in emergencies, can use a small petrol engine mounted on the gun to move short distances on the battlefield.

With a range of 24kms and a calibre of 155mm, the FH 70 is a considerable improvement on both the Abbot and M109. The gun is in service with West Germany (216), Italy (164), Saudi Arabia (72), Malaysia (30), Oman (12) and Japan (200).

105mm Light Gun

(212 in service). Crew 6: Weight 1,858kg: Length 8.8m: Width 1.78m: Height 21.3m: Ammunition HE, HEAT, WP, Smoke, Illuminating, Target Marking: Maximum Range (HE) 17.2kms: Anti Tank Range 800m: Muzzle Velocity 709m/s: Shell Weight HE 15.1kg: Rate of Fire 6rpm.

The Light Gun is in service with the UK Parachute and Commando Field Artillery Regiments as a go-anywhere, airportable weapon which can be carried around the battlefield underslung on a Puma or Chinook.

The gun was first delivered to the British Army in 1975 and since tht time it has replaced the older 105mm Pack Howitzer. A robust, reliable system, the gun proved its worth in the Falklands, where it is reported that guns were sometimes firing up to 400 rounds per day.

The Light Gun has been extremely successful in the international market with sales to Australia (59), Botswana (6), Brunei (6), Ireland (12), Kenya (40), Malawi (12), Malaysia (20), Morocco (36), New Zealand (34), Oman (39), Switzerland (6), UAE (50), United States (548) and Zimbabwe (12).

Javelin

(382 Fire Units in Service) Length 1.4m: Missile Diameter 76 cm: Missile Weight 11.1 kgs: Max Range 5.5kms: Warhead Weight 2.72 kgs: Max Altitude 3,000 feet: Max Speed Mach 1.7+: Fuse Proximity or Impact: Guidance SACLOS; Mount Man Portable.

Javelin is the British Army's successor to Blowpipe and is already in service with units in UKLF. It is an electronically more sophisticated system than Blowpipe with a greater range and a night sight. The greatest advantage is that it is now SACLOS guided, and all the operator has to do is keep the aiming mark on the target, leaving the guidance system to do the rest.

Javelin is believed to be a highly accurate system. Target practice during Javelin testing in 1985 presented the British Army with a problem regarding the numbers of available target drones. So many target drones were being destroyed during training that testing had to be slowed down until the manufacture of target drones caught up.

Javelin is deployed in armoured vehicles (Spartan or AFV 432) to provide point air defence for troops in the forward areas. A Javelin battery normally has 36 launchers.

In time we expect to see Javelin mounted on AAC helicopters and a naval version (Sea Javelin) is already available. In the longer term it is possible that Javelin may be entirely replaced by Starstreak in British service.

There is already considerable overseas interest in Javelin which is believed to cost about 60,000 pounds per missile at 1989 prices. Sales have already been made to Jordan and South Korea with potential customers believed to be Malaysia, Chile, Oman and Zimbabwe.

Javelin's predecessor Blowpipe achieved considerable success in the world market and we believe that over 30,000 missiles have been manufactured by 1990, with sales being made to the following - Canada, Chile, Ecuador, Malawi, Nigeria, Oman, Portugal, Qatar, and Thailand. Guerrilla forces in both Angola and Afghanistan are known to have acquired Blowpipe missiles.

Starstreak

(135 Fire Units on Order) Missile Length 1.39m: Missile Diameter 0.27m: Missile Speed Mach 4+: Maximum Range 7 kms: Minimum Range 300m.

Short Brothers of Belfast are the prime contractors for the Starstreak HVM (Hyper Velocity Missile) which continues along the development path of both Blowpipe and Javelin. The system can be shoulder launched using the LML (lightweight multiple launcher) or vehicle borne on the Alvis Stormer APC. The Stormer APC has an eight round launcher and 12 reload missiles can be carried inside the vehicle.

Starstreak which has been designed to counter threats from very high performance low flying aircraft and fast pop-up type strikes by attack helicopters, can easily be retrofitted to existing Blowpipe and Javelin equipment. The missile employs a system of three dart type projectiles which can make multiple hits on the target. Each of these darts has an explosive warhead combined with a chemical and kinetic energy penetrating shell. It is believed that the Starstreak has an SSK (single shot to kill) probability of over 95%.

During 1994 47 Regiment stationed at Thorney Island in the UK was issued with HVM mounted on Stormer. 47 Regiment supports 3 (UK) Division with batterys supporting brigades as follows:-

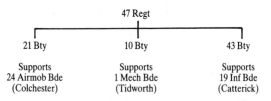

```
                              47 Regt
        ┌────────────────────────┼────────────────────────┐
     21 Bty                    10 Bty                    43 Bty

    Supports                  Supports                  Supports
  24 Airmob Bde              1 Mech Bde                19 Inf Bde
   (Colchester)              (Tidworth)                (Catterick)
```

Rapier

(120 fire units in service). Guidance Semi Automatic to line of Sight (SACLOS):
Missile Diameter 13.3 cm: Missile Length 2.35m: Rocket Solid Fuelled: Warhead
High Explosive: Launch Weight 42kg: Speed Mach 2+: Ceiling 3,000m: Maximum
Range 6,800m: Fire Unit Height 2.13m: Fire Unit Weight 1,227kg: Radar Height
(in action) 3.37m: Radar Weight 1,186kg: Optical Tracker Height 1.54m: Optical
Tracker Weight 119kg: Generator Weight 243kg: Generator Height 0.91m.

The Rapier system provides area, Low Level Air Defence (LLAD) over the
battlefield. It consists of an Optical Tracker, a Fire Unit, a Radar and a Generator.
The into-action time of the system is thought to be about 15 minutes and the radar
is believed to scan out to 12km. Each fire unit can therefore cover an Air Defence
Area (ADA) of about 100 square kms. Having discharged the 4 missiles on a Fire
Unit, 2 men are thought to be able to carry out a reload in about 3 minutes.

The Royal Artillery has 2 regiments equipped with Rapier, 1 in Germany with the
ARRC and one in UKLF. Each regiment has 3/4 batterys and each battery 10 fire
units. In the Falklands Campaign, Rapier was credited with 14 kills and 6 probables
from a total of 24 missiles fired.

We believe that three of the seven Rapier Batterys in service with the British Army
have been upgraded to Field Standard B2 (with Darkfire Electro optical tracker
and new surveillance radars).

In the longer term there will be a further upgrade to Field Standard C (known as
Rapier 2000) and that three batterys (31 fire units) of this equipment are currently
on order. The towed system launcher will mount eight missiles (able to fire two
simultaneously) which will be manufactured in two warhead versions. One of these
warheads will be armour piercing to deal with fixed wing targets, and the other a
fragmentation warhead for the engagement of cruise missiles and RPVs. Rapier
2000 will have the Darkfire tracker and a tailor made 3-dimensional radar system
for target acquisition developed by Plessey. The total cost of the Rapier FS"C"
programme is £1,886 million.

Rapier has now been sold to the armed forces of at least 14 nations. We believe that sales have amounted to over 25,000 missiles, 600 launchers and 350 Blindfire radars.

Tracked Rapier

(40 Fire Units in Service) Length 6.14m: Height 2.78m: Width 2.65m: Weight 13,381kg: Max Road Speed 61kph: Road Range 483kms: Engine GMFC Model 6V53 diesel: Engine Power 210hp, 2,800 rpm: Fuel Capacity 398 litres: Armament 8 Rapier Missiles: Vehicle Armour 25mm maximum: Reloads 20 missiles.

The Tracked Rapier system was originally developed for the Shah of Iran but after the revolution the order was cancelled and the British Army took over the contract. An original order to purchase 24 units was made in 1981, and with subsequent purchases there are currently approximately 40 units in service with one of the two Rapier Regiments.

There is no doubt that Tracked Rapier is a first class weapon system, and that mounting it on a modified US M548 chassis enhances its chances of survival on the battlefield with a considerable reduction in the normal into-action time. It is now possible for the forward tracked armoured units to continually operate under the cover of an ADA, which should make enemy close air support operations extremely difficult.

We believe that the Tracked Rapier in British service are the Mk 1B and are fitted with TOTE,(tracker, optical, thermally enhanced) guidance system, which enables the weapon to be used in all types of weather by day and by night.

Sound Ranging

Sound Ranging locates the positions of enemy artillery from the sound of their guns firing. Microphones are positioned on a line extending over a couple of kilometres to approximately 12 kilometers. As each microphone detects the sound of enemy guns firing the information is relayed to a Command Post which computes the location of the enemy battery. Enemy locations are then passed to Artillery Intelligence and counter battery tasks fired as necessary. Sound Ranging can identify an enemy position to within 50 metres at 10 kilometers.

MSTAR

Weight 30 kg: Wavelength J - Band: Range in excess of 20 kms.

MSTAR is a Lightweight Pulse Doppler J - Band All Weather Radar that has replaced the ZB 298 in the detection of helicopters, vehicles and infantry. Powered by a standard army field battery this radar will also assist the artillery observer in detecting the fall of shot. The electroluminescent display that shows dead ground relief and target track history, also has the ability to superimpose a map grid at the 1:50000 scale to ease transfer to military maps. MSTAR can be vehicle borne or broken down into three easily transportable loads for manpacking purposes.

Initial deliveries of MSTAR have been made to the Royal Artillery and these equipments will be used by Forward Observation Officers mounted in the Warrior Mechanised Artillery Observation Vehicle (MAOV). In time there should be over 100 MAOV equipped with MSTAR. MSTAR is believed to cost about £50,000 per unit at 1993 prices, and by the late 1990s we see a requirement for over 250 MSTAR equipments for use throughout the British Army.

COBRA

Cobra is a 3-D Phased Array Radar that is being developed for West Germany, France and the UK with a planned deployment date for the equipment towards the end of the decade. We currently expect West Germany to order 28 systems, France 15 and the UK 10. The current price estimate for a single equipment is in the region of £5 million at 1994 prices.

Until very recently companies involved in the Cobra project were forbidden to give details of the programme and information is still hard to obtain. What is known is that the equipment will be able to produce the locations of enemy artillery at extremely long ranges, and the radar will be able to cope with saturation type bombardments . In addition there will be a high degree of automated software, with high speed circuitry and secure data transmission to escape detection from enemy electronic countermeasures.

Cobra therefore appears to be an ideal equipment for operation in conjunction with MLRS. We would expect the British Army to field three Cobra Troops, each Troop consisting of three radars.

The first production models are now being built with troop trials expected in Germany during 1995/96. If orders are confirmed production is expected to peak at 14 radars per year in 1997 and run on until 2001. The British Army is currently looking at an in service date (ISD) of November 1998.

Cymbeline Mortar Locating Radar

(70 in service) Range 20kms: Weight of Radar 390kgs: Frequency I/J Band:

Cymbeline is the mortar locating radar which is currently under the command of the Close Support Regiments in both Germany and the UK. In Germany Cymbeline is mounted on an AFV 432 and in UKLF it is generally towed in a trailer. However with the advent of 3 (UK) Div it will almost certainly be carried on an APC.

Cymbeline detects the flight path of a mortar bomb at two points in the trajectory as it passes through the radar beam(s), rapid computing then enables the grid reference of the enemy base plate to be identified and engaged with artillery. An 81 mortar bomb can be detected at a range of about 10 kms while a 120mm bomb is detectable at about 14 kms.

Cymbeline first came into service with the British Army in 1973. Cymbeline will probably stay in service for some time to come and there is a possibility of a further Mark 4 upgrade to the present Mark 3 systems. Cymbeline will almost certainly be deployed with the AS 90 regiments when this gun appears in service.

In 1994 Cymbeline was deployed by the British Army in support of United Nations operations in the Sarajevo area of the Former Yugoslavia to identify gun and mortar positions around the city. The equipment appears to have been extremely successful in this role and has provided much valuable intelligence for the UN Command Staff.

At the beginning of 1995 we believe that over 350 Cymbeline were in service with 18 nations, including Singapore, Norway, Denmark, Finland, Oman, Saudi Arabia, Egypt, Kuwait, Nigeria, South Africa, Malawi, Switzerland and New Zealand.

Midge

Length 3.73m: Diameter 0.33m: Range approx 140kms: Operational Altitude 300-1,200m above launcher: Engine Williams WR2-6 single stage turbo-jet.

Midge is the battlefield reconnaissance, unmanned surveillance aircraft (RPV) in service with the Royal Artillery from the 1960s until very recently.

Midge is launched from a specially converted Bedford 4 ton vehicle, and flies along a preprogrammed flight path taking both conventional and infra-red photographs. The drone returns to the launch site after the mission, and when the engine shuts down, the drone descends by parachute and the film is recovered. A drone troop usually has two launchers and about 20 reload drones.

Midge is due to be replaced by the next generation RPV which is called Phoenix.

Phoenix

Phoenix is an all weather, day or night, real time surveillance system which consists of a variety of elements. It was developed under a contract initially awarded in 1985. The twin boom UAV (unmanned air vehicle) provides surveillance through its surveillance pod, the imagery from which is datalinked via a ground data terminal (GDT) to a ground control station (GCS). This controls the overall Phoenix mission and is used to distribute the UAV provided intelligence direct to artillery forces, to command level, or to a Phoenix troop command post (TCP). The principle method of communication from the GCS to artillery on the ground is via the battlefield artillery engagement system (BATES).

Powered by a 19kW (25hp) Target Technology 342 two stroke flat twin engine, the Phoenix air vehicle (with a centrally mounted fuel tank) is almost entirely manufactured from composites such as Kevlar, glass fibre, carbon reinforced plastics and Nomex honeycomb. The principal subcontractor is Flight Refueling of Christchurch in Dorset.

The modular design UAV can be launched within one hour of reaching a launch site and a second UAV can be dispatched within 8 minutes from the same launcher. The wing span is 5.5m and the maximum launch weight 175kgs. The manufacturer, GEC states that "Flight endurance is in excess of 4 hours, radius of action 50kms and the maximum altitude 2,700m (9,000 feet).

A flight section consists of a launch and recovery detachment and a ground control detachment. The launch and recovery detachment consists of three vehicles; the launch support vehicle, with several UAVs and mission pods in separate battlefield containers, plus operational replacement spares and fuel; the launch vehicle, which features a pallet-mounted lifting crane, the hydraulic catapult and launch ramp, a pre-launch detonator device, built-in test equipment, and the Land Rover recovery vehicle which is fitted with cradles for the air vehicle and mission pod. The ground-control detachment consists of two vehicles, the ground control station and the Land Rover towed ground data terminal.

The British Army has ordered three troops of Phoenix (approx 50 UAV) and believe that a troop will probably have about 10 - 15 UAV with associated ground support equipment. Of these three Phoenix troops, two will be operational and the third a reserve/training unit. The total cost of the programme is £203 million.

We believe that 57 (Bhurtpore) Locating Battery of 39 Regiment is being equipped with the first Phoenix units in early 1995. However, latest reports suggest continued 'in service' problems.

AMETS

An AMETS troop is responsible for providing the staff with up-to-date information regarding local weather conditions for use by artillery and NBC operators. AMETS troops are generally 20 strong, and the troop is usually part of a larger Locating Battery that has two other troops, one of which is dedicated to Sound Ranging and the other to unmanned surveillance aircraft operations.

With the extreme range of modern artillery and battlefield missiles, very precise calculations regarding wind and density are needed to ensure that the target is accurately engaged.

AMETS units can provide this information by releasing hydrogen filled balloons at hourly intervals recording important information on weather conditions at various levels of the atmosphere. The AMETS Troop travels in 4 ton box body vehicles.

(Air Defence Alerting System (ADAD))

An infra-red search and track system that is used by air defence units to detect hostile aircraft and helicopter targets and directs weapon systems into the target area. The air defence missile operators can be alerted to up to four targets in a priority order. The passive system which is built by Thorn EMI has an all weather, day and night capability.

Afterthought

> "Just send in your Chief an' surrender - it's worse if you fights or
> you runs: You can go where you please, you can shin up the trees,
> but you don't get away from the guns."

Rudyard Kipling

CHAPTER 7 - ARMY AVIATION

> *"Float like a butterfly - sting like a bee".*

> Muhammad Ali.

> *"Airpower is like poker. A second best hand is like none at all - it will cost you dough and win you nothing at all".*

> *General George C Kenney USAF.*

Army Air Corps

The Army obtains its aviation support from two agencies. The first is the Army Air Corps (AAC), which is an Army organisation with 5 separate regiments and a number of independent squadrons. The AAC also provides support for Northern Ireland on a mixed resident and roulement basis and the two squadrons concerned are sometimes referred to as the sixth AAC Regiment, although the units would disperse on mobilisation and have no regimental title.

By mid 1995 and following the "Options for Change" restructuring AAC regimental locations will be as follows:

1 Regiment	-	Germany
3 Regiment	-	Wattisham
4 Regiment	-	Wattisham
9 Regiment	-	Dishforth
7 Regiment	-	Netheravon

In addition to the Regiments in the UK and Germany there are small flights in Cyprus, Suffield (Canada) and the Falkland Islands. In Hong Kong 660 Sqn has 10 aircraft with a small detachment in Brunei.

The AAC Centre at Middle Wallop in Hampshire acts as a focal point for all Army Aviation, and it is here that the majority of training for pilots and aircrew is carried out.

Although the AAC operates some fixed wing aircraft for training, liaison flying and radar duties, the main effort goes into providing helicopter support for the ground forces. About 350 AAC helicopters are used for anti-tank operations, artillery fire control, reconnaissance, liaison flying and a limited troop lift.

Attack Helicopters

Army aviation is heavily involved in the battlefield revolution that was mentioned earlier in this publication. With the ability to move ground forces around the battlefield at speeds of up to 200kph and the proven ability of anti-tank helicopters to defeat tanks at 5,000m+, the helicopter has approached the point where it could be claimed to be one of the most important equipments on the battlefield. Both the Russians and the US have indicated their belief in the importance of the armed helicopter, and the Russians in particular believe that the armed helicopter has a superiority over the tank of 19:1, with the latest West German operational analysis figures suggesting that they believe that this superiority may be even higher.

During the 1991 Gulf War the US Army deployed 288 x AH-64 Apache in 15 Army Aviation battalions. The US Army claim that these aircraft destroyed 120 x APCs, 500 x MBT, 120 x Artillery Guns, 10 Radar Installations, 10 x Helicopters, 30 x Air Defence Units, about 300 soft skinned vehicles and 10 x fixed wing aircraft on the ground. A single Army Aviation AH-64 battalion is believed to have destroyed 40 x APCs and over 100 x MBT in an engagement that lasted over 3 hours, firing 107 Hellfire missiles and over 300 x 70mm rockets.

At the very beginning of the war 8 x AH-64 each equipped with 8 x Hellfire, 76 x 70mm rockets and 1,100 rounds of 30mm ammunition attacked radar early warning installations about 80-100 kms inside Iraq. Their task was to open a 30km wide sterilised air corridor through which allied aircraft could transit to targets deep inside enemy territory. During the operation the helicopters fired 27 x Hellfire missiles, 100 rockets and about 4,000 rounds of 30mm ammunition, achieving a very high success rate over a total distance of some 1,300 kms during the 15 hour mission.

What we are looking at is the natural progression of cavalry operations into another dimension. The 1980s aphorism "Rotors are to tanks as tracks were to horses" has not yet quite come to pass. Tracks, machine guns, and barbed wire drove horses from the modern battlefield. However, as the 20th century draws to a close, tanks, APCs, and other tracked vehicles are still very prominent and viable on that battlefield. Just as armour is most effective when supported by infantry, artillery, and even tactical air, helicopters are most effective when used in conjunction with, rather than in place of, armour and the other combat arms. However, helicopters so increase the range, mobility, reach, and vision of armoured forces, that they may be thought of as the latest manifestation of cavalry. Cavalry operations may be classed as light or heavy. In classic cavalry operations, heavy cavalry, as manifested by the mounted man-at-arms or Murat's Cavalry Corps, delivered shock and exploited penetrations. Confederate General JEB Stuart's operations in the first two years of the American Civil War typify light cavalry as a scouting and screening force. Lt Col Banastre Tarrelton's destruction of the defeated Carolina militia after the Battle of Cowpens, during the American War of Independence illustrates light cavalry in pursuit, while his less successful efforts against Francis Marion show some of the limitations in using light cavalry to control insurgents.

Indeed, the division persisted into armoured operations. Heavy armour provided shock, penetration, and exploitation or pursuit, while scouting, screening, and the control of insurgents were the province of light armour. Attack or combat helicopters are roughly analogous to heavy cavalry. Their heavy armament provides shock and limits the enemy's freedom of operation, while their defensive and protective features enable them to operate in the thick of the modern battlefield or strike deep behind enemy lines. Lighter helicopters, while often armed, lack the survivability of their heavier brethren. Consequently, they must operate from concealment or from behind friendly lines. Thus, they inherit the light cavalry roles of scouting and observation.

However, it would be wise to take all of these recent changes in their turn and not "go overboard" on any one particular system. The attack helicopter is going to be an increasingly important battlefield system in the years to come, but it is part of a whole and not a battle winner in isolation.

In its turn the helicopter is already threatened. To ensure survival helicopters fly close to the "nap of the earth" (NOE) and hide behind features such as woods and small hills. The race is on to produce effective anti-helicopter mines that recognise friend from foe, and either destroy low flying helicopters operating along likely transit routes, or force them to fly higher where they become vulnerable to missiles and anti-aircraft fire. Plans for large procurements of anti-helicopter mines are already in place in the US and many European Union (EU) nations.

We believe that there are approximately 11,700 helicopters, armed to some degree, in current world service. Of these, about 4,200 may be classed as attack helicopters and of these 4,200, some 1,600 are in service with the US Army (1,500) and US Marine Corps (100).

AAC Attack Helicopter Replacement

The current attack helicopter in service with the AAC is Lynx with TOW, and will almost certainly continue to be so until December 1997 which is the in service date (ISD) for the British Army's new attack helicopter.

By mid 1995 the announcement should have been made as to which aircraft has won the British Army's current attack helicopter competition. There are currently four aircraft under consideration for the 93 aircraft contract:

	Unit Cost Estimate
AH-64/D Apache (McDonnell Douglas/Westland)	£21 million
Tiger (Eurocopter/BAe)	£30 million
Cobra Venom (Bell/GEC-Marconi)	£14 million
Rooivalk (Atlas Aviation/Marshall Aerospace)	£12 million

The competition is by now (April 1995) too far adanced to speculate upon. The decision has almost certainly been made and probably only requires Cabinet approval. Suffice to say that the operational effectiveness of the aircraft is not the only criteria upon which the final judgement is being made. Cost is an extremely important consideration and political considerations are vital. Whatever happens during the next few months, we are now almost 100% certain that the British Army will have a dedicated attack helicopter in service by the end of the decade.

In the run up towards the procurement of an attack helicopter fleet, during recent exercises, Army Air Corps crews practised Joint Air Attack Team (JAAT) procedures developed from operational experience gained during the Gulf War. The JAAT team concept is a combination of offensive air support, army aviation elements and integrated artillery support which produces a highly mobile force with an awesome destructive capability. Although the JAAT team concept has not yet been officially adopted as tactical doctrine by the British Army, the concept is a valuable pointer of the direction in which operational planning is moving. In the longer term JAAT type operations will probably become accepted as the norm.

On a lighter note we believe that by the end of the decade our projections suggest that the number of helicopters in service with the British Army will be greater than the number of horses on strength.

Support Helicopters

The majority of the troop lift and logistical support for military operations is provided by the RAF who currently operate approximately 130 support helicopters (Wessex, Puma, Chinook), and there are excellent reasons to support proposals which suggest that these aircraft should be under AAC command and control. This system may not work as well as it might because of differences in operational procedures linked to traditional service attitudes and priorities. We firmly believe that an army commander on the ground should command all the battlefield assets at his disposal including troop lift helicopters and their crews. The British Army is the one remaining major NATO Army where the Army Commander does not have total command and control over his helicopter fleet. Allowing such a situation to continue to exist could invite confusion in a crisis situation.

AAC Regimental Organisation

Organisations for the individual AAC Regiments appear to be in a state of flux. The following wiring diagram outlines the organisation of 3 Regiment AAC in early 1995. 3 Regiment supports the Colchester based 24 Airmobile Brigade. Various regimental organisations are a variation on this theme.

```
                         3 Regiment AAC
                           (Wattisham)

                            Regtl HQ
                     (Commander-Lt Colonel)
        ┌──────────────┬──────────────────┬──────────────┐
   662 Sqn          653 Sqn           663 Sqn          HQ Sqn
6 x Lynx with TOW  11 x Lynx     6 x Lynx with Tow   REME LAD
   6 x Gazelle                      6 x Gazelle         Admin
                                                         Sigs
                                                          QM
```

Totals: Approx 450 personnel
        35 Helicopters

Notes:

(1) A Regiment of this type could act as the core formation of an airborne
battlegroup. If necessary an infantry aviation company conisting of 3 x rifle
platoons and a Milan anti-tank platoon will be attached. The infantry could be
moved in RAF Chinooks or Pumas.

(2) 4 Regiment AAC join 3 Regiment in Wattisham during early 1995 and we
believe that both regiments will have a similar organisation. Wattisham is also the
home of 7 Bn REME - a unit configured as an aircraft workshops.

RAF Support

As previously mentioned the second agency that provides aviation support for the
Army is the Royal Air Force. In general terms the RAF provides helicopters that
are capable of moving troops and equipment around the battlefield, and fixed wing
fighter ground attack (FGA) aircraft that provide close air support to the troops in
the vicinity of the Forward Edge of the Battlefield Area (FEBA). The RAF also
provides the heavy air transport aircraft that will move men and material from one
theatre of operations to another.

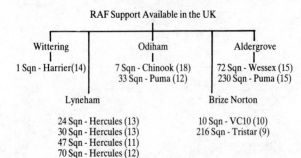

RAF Support Available in the UK

Wittering
1 Sqn - Harrier(14)

Odiham
7 Sqn - Chinook (18)
33 Sqn - Puma (12)

Aldergrove
72 Sqn - Wessex (15)
230 Sqn - Puma (15)

Lyneham
24 Sqn - Hercules (13)
30 Sqn - Hercules (13)
47 Sqn - Hercules (11)
70 Sqn - Hercules (12)

Brize Norton
10 Sqn - VC10 (10)
216 Sqn - Tristar (9)

(1) Figures in brackets are our estimate of the number of aircraft in each squadron during early 1995.

(2) A further 16 x Harrier are available with the Operational Conversion Unit (OCU) at RAF Wittering. This OCU has the mobilisation title of 20 (R) Sqn.

(3) Not shown on the above diagram but available for support if necessary are 26 x Tornado GR1A (12 Sqn & 617 Sqn) and 43 x Jaguar GR1A (6,41 & 54 Sqns).

RAF Support Available
British Forces Germany
2 Group RAF

Laarbruch
3 Sqn - Harrier (13)
4 Sqn - Harrier (13)
18 Sqn - Chinook (5)
& Puma (5)

Bruggen
9 Sqn - Tornado GR1 (13)
14 Sqn - Tornado GR1 (13)
17 Sqn - Tornado GR1 (13)
31 Sqn - Tornado GR1 (13)

Note: Figures in brackets are our estimate of the number of aircraft in each squadron during early 1995.

We would expect the AAC armed helicopter to deal with the localised armoured threats to a British force on operations. We would expect RAF aircraft to be used on targets of regimental size (90 tanks) and above. However, high performance modern aircraft are very expensive and fast jet pilots take up to 3 years to train. It would only be sensible to risk such valuable systems when all other options had failed. In addition, the strength of enemy air defences would probably allow only one pass to be made over the target area. A second pass by fixed wing aircraft after ground defences had been alerted would be almost suicidal.

AAC Aircraft

Lynx AH - Mark 1/7/9

(126 in service). Length Fuselage 12.06m: Height 3.4m: Rotor Diameter 12.8m:
Max Speed 330kph: Cruising Speed 232kph: Range 885km: Engines 2 Rolls-Royce
Gem 41: Power 2 x 850 bhp: Fuel Capacity 918 litres(internal): Weight (max take
off) 4,763kg: Crew one pilot, one air-gunner/observer: Armament 8 x TOW
Anti-Tank Missiles: 2-4 7.62mm machine guns: Passengers-able to carry 10 PAX:
Combat radius approx 100kms with 2 hour loiter.

Lynx is the helicopter used by the British Army to counter the threat posed by
enemy armoured formations. Armed with 8 x TOW missiles the Lynx is now the
mainstay of the British armed helicopter fleet. However, in addition to its role as an
anti-tank helicopter, Lynx can be used for fire support using machine guns, troop
lifts, casualty evacuation and many more vital battlefield tasks.

During hostilities we would expect Lynx to operate on a section basis, with 2 or 3
Lynx aircraft armed with TOW directed by a Section Commander possibly flying in
a Gazelle. The Section Commander would control what is in reality an airborne
tank ambush and following an attack on enemy armour decide when to break
contact. Having broken contact, the aircraft would return to a forward base to
refuel and rearm. Working from forward bases, some of which are within 10kms of
the FEBA, it is suggested that a Lynx section could be "turned around" in less than
15 minutes. Lynx with TOW replaced SCOUT with SS11 as the British Army's
anti-tank helicopter.

We believe the majority of Lynx in British service to be Lynx Mark 7 and that there
are currently 24 Lynx Mark 9 (the latest version) in the inventory.

Lynx is known to be in service with France, Brazil, Argentina, The Netherlands,
Qatar, Denmark, Norway, West Germany and Nigeria. The naval version carries
anti-ship missiles.

TOW 2B

(Tube Launched, Optically Tracked, Wire Guided, Anti-Tank Missile). Length
1.17m: Diameter 15cm: Maximum Range 3750m: Speed 1127khp (200mps):
Warhead 3.9kg shaped charge high explosive HEAP : Missile Weight 28.1kg:
Guidance Automatic command to line of sight: Armour Penetration 800mm.

TOW is the US system that has been adopted for use on the Lynx anti-tank helicopter. First seen in US service in 1965 TOW is a very powerful system that can defeat the armour on all conventional MBTs. It is also a second generation missile in that the operator no longer "flies" the missile to the target using a control stick. All the operator needs to do is keep the aiming mark on the target and the guidance system will do the rest. AAC Lynx are fitted with the roof-mounted stabilised M65 sight.

TOW 2B is the top attack version of the missile system and these systems in AAC service are being upgraded under the Further Improved Tow Programme which enhances both range (possibly 5,000m) and armour penetration.

Scout

(69 on inventory). Fuselage Length 9.33m: Height 2.71m: Width 1.65m: Rotor Diameter 9.83m: Max Speed 210kph: Cruising Speed 196kph: Range 507kms: Engines Rolls-Royce Bristol minibus 102: Power 710bhp: Fuel Capacity 709 litres: Weight 2,404kg Crew Pilt plus air gunner/observer + 2 pax: Armament 4 + SS 11 Missiles; 2 x 7.62 machine guns.

In service with the AAC since 1962 Scout has been replaced as the Army's main anti-tank helicopter by Lynx. A rugged, versatile aircraft Scout carried the French SS 11 missile with a maximum range of 3,000m as its main armament.

Scout has been used in almost every battlefield role during its service and we expect a few to remain with the AAC for training and liaison flying now that the Lynx re-equipment programme is complete. The early 1995 count suggests that some 30 remain in squadron service.

Gazelle

(159 in service). Fuselage Length 9.53m: Height 3.18m: Rotor Diameter 10.5m: Maximum Speed 265kph: Cruising Speed 233kph: Range 670km: Engine Turbomeca/Rolls-Royce Astazou 111N: Power 592shp: Fuel Capacity 445 litres: Weight 1,800kg (max take off): Armament 2 x 7.62mm machine guns (not a standard fitting).

Gazelle is the general purpose helicopter in use by the AAC and it is capable of carrying out a variety of battlefield roles. Gazelle is a French design built under licence by Westland Aircraft. Over 1,000 Gazelles are in service with air forces and civil aviation organisations throughout the world.

(A-109)

(4 in service). Fuselage Length 10.7m: Rotor Diameter 11.0m: Cruising Speed 272kph: Range 550kms: Service Ceiling 4570m: Engines 2 x 420-shp Allison 250-C20B turboshafts: Fuel Capacity 560 litres: Weight 1,790kg: Max Take Off Weight 2600 kg: Crew - Pilot plus observer + 7 pax:

The AAC has four of these light general purpose aircraft for liaison flying and special tasks. The aircraft are part of 8 Flight based at Netheravon in Wiltshire.

BN-2 Islander

(7 In Service) Crew 2; Length Overall 12.37m; Max Take Off Weight 3,630 kg; Max Cruising Speed at 2,135m (7,000 ft and 75% of power) 257kph (154mph); Ceiling 4,145m (13,600m); Range at 2,137m (7,000ft and 75% of power) 1,153km (717 miles); Range with Optional Tanks 1,965kms (1,221 miles).

The AAC's BN-2 Islanders carry the Thorn EMI CASTOR (Corps Airborne Stand Off Radar) that is designed to provide intelligence information in the forward edge of the battlefield (FEBA) and beyond while operating well within friendly territory. The radar, located in the nose cone of the aircraft has a 360 degree scan and offers wide coverage against moving and static targets.

Chipmunk T Mark 10
(21 In Service) Crew 2; Length 7.8m; Span 10.3m; Height 2.13m; Max Speed 222 km/ph (138mph); Engine 1 x 1DH Gipsy Major 8 Piston Engine.

The world famous Chipmunk is currently used to give air experience/basic flying training to potential AAC pilots. These aircraft were initially taken into service with the RAF in 1950 and we are sure that it will be some considerable time before they disappear from service. At the height of the "Cold War" the RAF's permanent presence in Berlin was a flight of 2 x Chipmunks, a presence that we are assured was not directly responsible for the collapse of the Warsaw Pact.

RAF Aircraft

Puma

In Service With:

18 Sqn	5 x Puma HC1	RAF Laarbruch
33 Sqn	12 x Puma HC1	RAF Odiham
230 Sqn	15 x Puma HC1	RAF Aldergrove
OCU	5 x Puma HC1	RAF Odiham

Crew 2 or 3; Fuselage Length 14.06m; Width 3.50m; Height 4.38m; Weight (empty) 3,615kg; Maximum Take Off Weight 7,400kgs; Cruising Speed 258 km/ph (192mph); Service Ceiling 4,800m; Range 550kms; 2 x Turbomecca Turmo 111C4 turbines.

The "package deal" between the UK and France on helicopter collaboration dates back to February 1967 when Ministers of the two countries signed a Memorandum of Understanding (MOU). The programme covered the development of three helicopter types - the Puma, Gazelle and Lynx. The main contractors engaged on the programme were Westland and SNIAS for the airframe, and Rolls Royce and Turbomeca for the engines.

Development of the Puma was already well advanced in France when collaboration began. However, the flight control system has been developed jointly by the two countries, and a great deal of work done by Westland to adapt the helicopter for the particular operational requirements of the RAF. Production of the aircraft was shared between the two countries, the UK making about 20% by value of the airframe, slightly less for the engine as well as assembling the aircraft procured for the RAF. Deliveries of the RAF Pumas started in 1971.

The Puma is powered by 2 x Turbomeca Turmo 111C4 engines mounted side by side above the main cabin. Capable of many operational roles Puma can carry 16 fully equipped troops, or 20 at light scales. In the casualty evacuation role (CASEVAC), 6 stretchers and 6 sitting cases can be carried. Underslung loads of up to 3,200kgs can be transported over short distances and an infantry battalion can be moved using 34 Puma lifts.

Chinook

In Service With:

7 Sqn	18 x Chinook	HC1 RAF Odiham
18 Sqn	5 x Chinook HC1	RAF Laarbruch
27 Sqn (R) (OCU)	4 x Chinook HC1	RAF Odiham
78	Sqn Chinook HC1	RAF MPA (Falklands)

Crew 4; Fuselage Length 15.54m; Width 3.78m; Height 5.68m; Weight (empty) 10,814kgs; Internal Payload 8,164kgs; Rotor Diameter 18.29m; Cruising Speed 270 km/ph (158mph); Service Ceiling 4,270m; Mission Radius (with internal and external load of 20,000kgs including fuel and crew) 55kms; Rear Loading Ramp Heigth 1.98m; Rear Loading Ramp Width 2.31m; Engines 2 x Avco Lycoming T55-L11E turboshafts.

The Chinook HC1 is a tandem-rotored, twin-engined medium lift helicopter. It has a crew of four (pilot, navigator and 2 x crewmen) and is capable of carrying 45 fully equipped troops or a variety of heavy loads up to approximately 10 tons. The first Chinooks entered service with the RAF in 1982.

The triple hook system allows greater flexibility in load carrying and enables some loads to be carried faster and with greater stability. In the ferry configuration with internally mounted fuel tanks, the Chinook'srange is over 1,600 kms (1,000 miles). In the medical evacuation role the aircraft can carry 24 x stretchers.
Chinook aircraft are currently being upgraded to the HC2 standard. The first of the 32 aircraft being upgraded was delivered to the RAF in the Spring of 1993, with the remaining aircraft due to be modified by the end of 1995. The HC2 upgrade, for which a total of £145 million has been allocated (£53 million during 1993/94), allows for the aircraft to be modified to the US CH-47D standard with some extra enhancements. These enhancements include fitting infra-red jammers, missile approach warning indicators, chaff and flare dispensers, a long range fuel system and machine gun mountings.
This is a rugged and reliable aircraft. During the Falklands War reports suggest that, at one stage 80 fully equipped troops were carried in one lift and, during a Gulf War mission a single Chinook carried 110 Iraqui POWs. The Chinook mid-life update will significantly enhance the RAF's ability to support the land forces during the next 25 years.

Since 1 April 1990 the RAF Chinook fleet has flown some 44,200 hours during which time the operating costs (personnel, fuel and maintenance) have been £232 million, a figure that results in a cost of £5,248 per flying hour. On average 18 of the 32 aircraft have been available for front-line service at any one time. This figure reflects the need for planned maintenance and servicing. On 9 March 1995 the UK MOD announced a purchase of a further 14 x Chinooks and a separate buy of 22 x EH-101.

Westland Wessex Mark 2

(54 in service - possibly 30 earmarked for Army support). Crew 1-3; Pax 16 in main cabin: Length 20.03m: Main Rotor Diameter 17.07m: Height 4.93m: Cabin Door Size 1.22m x 1.22m: Operating Weight Mk2 3,767kg: Payload Mk2 1,117kg: Max Speed 212kph: Cruising Speed 195kph: Max Range 770km.

The first production model of the Wessex Mk2 was delivered to the RAF in 1962, and until the introduction of Puma the Wessex Mk 2 was the most numerous transport helicopter in service with the British Forces. It is believed that the RAF now operates one Wessex Mk2 squadron which supports UKLF (72 Sqn - RAF Aldergrove - 15 aircraft), a Wessex squadron in service with the RAF in Cyprus (No 84 Sqn - RAF Akrotiri - possibly 5/6 aircraft) and another in Hong Kong (28 Sqn - RAF Sek Kong - 8 aircraft). Other marks of Wessex are used by the RAF for Search and Rescue and by the Royal Navy for antisubmarine warfare.

Harrier

In Service With:

1 Sqn	14 x Harrier GR7	RAF Wittering
3 Sqn	13 x Harrier GR7	RAF Laarbruch
4 Sqn	13 x Harrier GR7	RAF Laarbruch
20 Sqn (R) OCU*	16 x Harrier	RAF Wittering

* There appear to be a mix of aircraft at the OCU. We believe that there could be Harrier GR3, GR5/7 and up to 10 x Harrier T4.

Crew (GR 5/7) 1; (T Mark 4 & 4A) 2; Length (GR 5/7) 14m; Length (T Mark 4 & 4A) 17m; Wingspan (normal) 9.3m; Height (GR 5/7) 3.45m; Height (T Mark 4 & 4A) 4.17m; Max Speed 1083 km/ph (673mph) at sea level; All Up Operational Weight approx 13,494kgs; Armament 2 x 30mm Aden guns, 4 x wing weapon pylons and 1 x underfuselage weapon pylon, conventional or cluster bombs; Engine 1 x Rolls-Royce Pegasus 11-21; Ferry Range 5,382 kms (3,310 miles) with 4 x drop tanks.

Capable of taking off and landing vertically, the Harrier is not tied to airfields with long concrete runways but can be dispersed to sites in the field close to the forward edge of the battle area. The normal method of operation calls for a short take off and vertical landing (STOVL), as a short ground roll on take off enables a greater weapon load to be carried. The Harrier GR3 was the mark of the aircraft that was taken into service in large numbers starting in 1969.

The Harrier GR5 entered service in 1988 with the intention of replacing all of the RAF's GR3's on a one for one basis. However, the GR5 has been upgraded to the GR7, which in turn entered service in June 1990. All three of the operational Harrier squadrons have been equipped with the GR7 and all of the GR3s and GR5s have either been upgraded or withdrawn from service.

The differences in the GR5 and the GR7 are mainly in the avionics. The GR7 is equipped with the Forward Looking Infra Red (FLIR) equipment which, when combined with the night vision goggles (NVGs) that the pilot will wear, gives the GR7 a night, low level, poor weather capability. There are small differences in the cockpit of the two aircraft including layout and internal lighting standards. In most other respects, the GR7 is similar to the GR5.

The GR5/7 offers many advantages over the GR3. It possesses the capability to carry approximately twice the weapon load over the same radius of action, or the same weapon load over a much increased radius. In addition it carries a comprehensive ECM (Electronic Counter Measures) suite which can operate in the passive or active mode and will greatly enhance the GR5/7s chances of survival in today's high threat environment. The GR5/7 also has an inertial navigation system that is significantly more effective than that of the GR3.

C-130 Hercules

In Service With:

24 Sqn	13 x Hercules C1P/C3P/C1K	RAF Lyneham
30 Sqn	13 x Hercules C1/C3/C1K	RAF Lyneham
47 Sqn	11 x Hercules C1/C3	RAF Lyneham
70 Sqn	12 x Hercules	RAF Lyneham
57 Sqn (R) OCU	5 x Hercules	RAF Lyneham

Note: The LTW appears to have a total of 54 aircraft. The squadron totals are given as a guide to what we believe are the average aircraft figures per squadron and the OCU at any one time.

Crew 5; Capacity 92 troops or 62 paratroops or 74 medical litters or 19,686kgs of freight; Length 29.78m; Span 40.41m; Height 11.66m; Weight Empty 34,287kgs; Max Load 45,093kgs; Max speed 618 km/ph (384mph); Service Ceiling 13,075m; Engines 4 x Allison T-56A-15 turboprops.

The Hercules C1 is the workhorse of the RAF transport fleet. It has proved to be a versatile and rugged aircraft, primarily intended for tactical operations, including troop carrying, paratrooping, supply dropping and aeromedical duties. The Hercules can operate from short unprepared airstrips, but also possesses the endurance to mount long range strategic lifts if required. The aircraft is a derivative of the C-130E used by the United States Air Force, but is fitted with British Avionic equipment, a roller-conveyor system for heavy air-drops and with more powerful engines. The crew of five includes, pilot, co-pilot, navigator, air engineer and air loadmaster.

As a troop carrier, the Hercules can carry 92 fully armed men, while for airborne operations 62 paratroops can be dispatched in two simultaneous "sticks" through the fuselage side doors. Alternatively, 40 paratroops can jump from the rear loading ramp. As an air ambulance the aircraft can accommodate 74 stretchers.

Freight loads that can be parachuted from the aircraft include: 16 x 1 ton containers or 4 x 8,000 pound platforms or 2 x 16,000 pound platforms or 1 x platform of 30,000 pounds plus. Amongst the many combinations of military loads that can be carried in an air-landed operation are: 3 x Ferret scout cars plus 30 passengers or 2 x Land Rovers and 30 passengers or 2 x Gazelle helicopters.

Of the original 66 C1 aircraft, some 31 have been given a fuselage stretch producing the Mark C3. The C3 "stretched version" provides an additional 37% more cargo space. Refuelling probes have been fitted above the cockpit of both variants and some have received radar warning pods under the wing tips. One aircraft, designated Mark W2, is a special weather version and is located at the DRA Farnborough.

RAF Hercules are currently assisting in airlifting aid in support of UN operations in many areas of the world. For example, working from a forward airhead at Ancona on the eastern coast of Italy, a detachment of 38 officers and men with a single Hercules from 47 Sqn, averaged almost three flights a day for the year 3 July 1992 - 3 July 1993. Over 900 sorties lifted more than 19 million pounds of freight into Sarajevo. The aircraft were flown by six crews on a two week rotation from RAF Lyneham.

Current plans appear to be for the replacement of the RAF's ageing 1960s Hercules fleet during the next ten years and the UK MOD recently announced the purchase of 25 x C-130J from Lockheed. This aircraft has improved engines, a new glass cockpit with flat screen displays and a two man crew. The first test and demonstrator aircraft are expected to be flying in September 1995 with production models available from the middle of 1996.

Orders for a second batch of 30 transport aircraft are believed to be in the system towards the end of the decade and the contenders will probably be Lockheed once again with a C-130 built to a new K standard and the FLA (future large aircraft). The FLA which will be built by the Rome based Euroflag Consortium, will probably be ready for service from about 2004 and could be capable of carrying a maximum payload of 30 tons as opposed to the 20 tons of the C-130J. British Aerospace is a member of Euroflag consortium.

The most commonly quoted argument in favour of the FLA is that this aircraft could carry a 25 ton payload over a distance of 4,000kms. Thus it is argued that a fleet of 40 x FLA could carry a UK Brigade to the Gulf within 11.5 days, as opposed to the 28.5 days required to make a similar deployment with 40 x C-130s.

Over 1,000 x C-130 have been manufactured and 467 are in service with the US Armed Forces.

Tristar

(9 in service with 216 Sqn) Crew 3; Passengers 265 and 35,000 pounds of freight; Length 50.05m; Height 16.87m; Span 47.35m; Max Speed 964 km/ph (600mph); Range 6,000 miles (9,600 kms); Engines 3 x 22,680kgs thrust Rolls Royce RB 211-524B4 turbofans.

The Tristar K1 and KC1 are strategic tanker conversions of the Lockheed

L-1011-500 Tristar commercial airliner. The Tristar K1 can also be fitted with up to 204 passenger seats for the trooping role. The Tristar KC1 tanker/freight aircraft have a large 140 x 102 inch, cargo door and a roller conveyor system capable of accepting up to 20 cargo pallets or seating for up to 196 passengers. Linked pallets can be used to permit the carriage of vehicles.

Also in service is the Tristar C2. This aircraft can carry 265 passengers and 35,000 pounds of freight over ranges in excess of 4,000 miles. It is planned to give these aircraft a tanker capability by fitting two wing refuelling pods.

The Tristar normally cruises at 525mph and with a payload of 50,000 pounds has a range in excess of 6,000 miles. The aircraft entered service in early 1986 with No 216 Sqn which reformed at RAF Brize Norton on 1 Nov 1984.

VC-10

(19 in service with 10 Sqn and 101 Sqn) Crew 4; Carries 150 passengers or 78 medical litters; Height 12.04m; Span 44.55m ; Length 48.36m; Max Speed (425 mph); Range 7596kms; All Up Operational Weight 146,513kgs; Engines 4 x Rolls Royce Conway turbofans.

The VC-10 is a fast transport aircraft which is the backbone of Strike Command's long-range capability, providing flexibility and speed of deployment for British Forces. This multi-purpose aircraft can be operated in the troop transport, freight and aeromedical roles in addition to maintaining scheduled air services.

The VC-10 carries a flight deck crew of four - captain, co-pilot, navigator and engineer - and has a flight deck seat for an additional supernumerary crew member. Normal cabin staff are two air loadmasters and two air stewards. On scheduled services up to 126 passengers are carried. Under the floor of the aircraft are two large holds which can carry up to 8.5 tons of freight. If necessary, the aircraft can be converted for use as a freighter or an air ambulance when 78 stretcher cases can be carried. Five aircraft are used as airborne refueling tankers.

Future Support Helicopters

During early March 1995 the Secretary of State for Defence announced the UK Government's intention to purchase a further 14 x Boeing CH-47 Chinook (bringing the in-service CH-47 total to 46) and 22 x Westland EH101. We believe that current plans are for the EH101 to be operated by the RAF.

The EH101 is a joint project with Augusta of Italy and the aircraft is the land forces version of the naval Merlin helicopter. EH101 can carry 4.5 tons of freight, 30 troops at light scales, has a range of 926 kms and a cruising speed of 276 kph. Running costs for EH101 are £750 per hour as opposed to the CH-47 running costs of £1,000 per hour. The aircraft has three engines as opposed to the two of the

CH-47, is more crash resistant and has a significantly small radar cross section that will enhance its battlefield survivability.

The UK MOD believes that a purchase of EH101 will retain over 1,800 jobs in Britain during the next 10 years and that there is considerable potential for export sales, particularly in the Middle East.

CHAPTER 8 - ENGINEERS

"I hope it doesn't thunder Sir, or I'll be really frightened".

Sapper to his Troop Commander (573 Field Company) during the clearance of a minefield lane at the start of the Battle of Alamein. Mines were being cleared by hand, at night, under heavy machine gun fire and an artillery barrage. Some of the anti-tank mines had been booby trapped to make handling more difficult.

Corps of Royal Engineers

The engineer support for the Army is provided by the Corps of Royal Engineers (RE). This large corps, currently composed of 21 regiments filled with highly skilled tradesmen is currently organised as follows:

	Germany	UKLF	Hong Kong
Engineer Regiments	5	4	-
EOD Regiment	-	1	-
Resident N Ireland Regiment	-	1	-
Gurkha Engineer Regiment	-	-	1
TA Engineer Regiments	-	9	-

There are also a number of independent engineer squadrons world-wide. The Gurkha Engineer Regiment will reduce to a large squadron following the withdrawal from Hong Kong in 1997.

The Royal Engineers provide specialist support to the combat formations and engineer detachments can be found at all levels from the Combat Team/Company Group upwards. Combat Engineers could be expected to be involved in the following tasks during specific phases of warfare:

a. Defence: Constructon of field defences; minelaying; improvement and construction of obstacles.

b. Attack: Obstacle crossing; demolition of enemy defences (bunkers etc); mine clearance; bridge or ferry construction.

c. Advance: Building or strengthening roads and bridges; removal of booby traps; mine clearance; airfield construction; supply of water; survey.

d. Withdrawal: Demolition - of airfields, roads and bridges, fuel ammunition and food dumps, railway tracks and rolling stock,industrial plant and facilities such as power stations; route clearance; minelaying; booby trapping likely enemy future positions and items that might be attractive to the enemy. Some of the other tasks performed by the men of the RE include map making and survey, the disposal of air launched enemy weapons (bombs etc), airfield damage repair and advice to other arms on camouflage and concealment. Often amongst the first soldiers into battle, and still involved in dangerous tasks such as mine clearance in the areas such as Cambodian and the former Yugoslavia, the Sappers can turn their hands to almost any engineering task.

Recent UN peacekeeping tasks have highlighted the importance of combat engineers in all spheres of military activity. During 1994 the multitude of tasks for which engineer support was requested stretched the resources of the Corps to its limit and the first priority in any call from the UN for support is for engineers. Tracks have to be improved, roads must be built, wells dug and clean water provided together with camps for refugees. All of these are engineer tasks that soak up large amounts of manpower.

Organisations

The smallest engineer unit is the field troop which is usually commanded by a Lieutenant and consists of approximately 44 men. In an armoured division a field troop can be expected to have up to four sections and each section is mounted in an APC. Engineer Regiments in UKLF may have only three sections and may be mounted in wheeled vehicles such as Land Rovers and 4 Ton Trucks. An engineer troop will carry equipment, stores and explosives to enable it to carry out its immediate battlefield tasks.

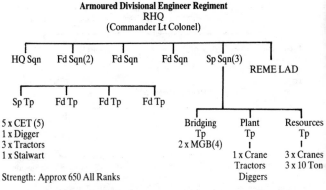

Armoured Divisional Engineer Regiment
RHQ
(Commander Lt Colonel)

HQ Sqn	Fd Sqn(2)	Fd Sqn	Fd Sqn	Sp Sqn(3)

REME LAD

Sp Tp   Fd Tp   Fd Tp   Fd Tp

5 x CET (5)
1 x Digger
3 x Tractors
1 x Stalwart

Bridging Tp
2 x MGB(4)

Plant Tp
1 x Crane
Tractors
Diggers

Resources Tp
3 x Cranes
3 x 10 Ton

Strength: Approx 650 All Ranks

(1) This Regiment would send most of its soldiers to man the engineer detachments that provide support for a division's battlegroups; (2) Field Squadron (expect a field squadron to have approximately 68 vehicles and some 200 men; (3) Support Squadron; (4) Medium Girder Bridge; (5) Combat Engineer Tractor; (6) This

105

whole organisation is highly mobile and built around the AFV 432 and Spartan series of vehicles; (7) In addition to the regimental REME LAD each squadron has its own REME section of approximately 12 - 15 men.

An Engineer field troop assigned to work in support of a Battlegroup operating in the area of the FEBA could be expected to resemble the following:-

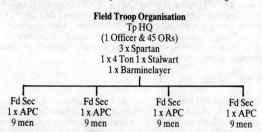

Field Troop Organisation
Tp HQ
(1 Officer & 45 ORs)
3 x Spartan
1 x 4 Ton 1 x Stalwart
1 x Barminelayer

Fd Sec	Fd Sec	Fd Sec	Fd Sec
1 x APC	1 x APC	1 x APC	1 x APC
9 men	9 men	9 men	9 men

Engineer amphibious capability and specialist support is provided by elements of 28 Engineer Regiment in Germany and a TA Regiment in the UK. The current organisation of 28 Regiment resembles the following.

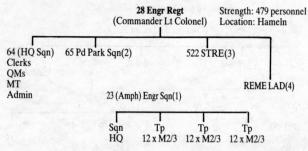

28 Engr Regt Strength: 479 personnel
(Commander Lt Colonel) Location: Hameln

64 (HQ Sqn)   65 Pd Park Sqn(2)   522 STRE(3)
Clerks
QMs
MT   REME LAD(4)
Admin

23 (Amph) Engr Sqn(1)

| Sqn HQ | Tp 12 x M2/3 | Tp 12 x M2/3 | Tp 12 x M2/3 |

(1) We would expect 23 Amphibious Engineer Squadron with about 170 men to have 36 x M2 Ferries (to be replaced by M3 in 1996-97); (2) 65 Field Park Squadron acts as the theatre engineering resource unit and as well as manufacturing and repairing equipment, holds the equipment required by all RE units in Germany. The squadron has about 100 military and 150 civilian staff. (3) 522 Specialist Team Royal Engineers (STRE) is a small team (approx 26 strong) which provides a service resembling design consultancy for specific engineering tasks. (4) The REME LAD has three repair platoons and a strength of 152 personnel. (5) On mobilisation 28 Engr Regt would take 2 x Field Squadrons from 35 Engineer

Regiment (also in Hameln) under command and 21 Field Squadron (EOD) from 33 Engr Regiment in the UK.

The UK Engineer Field Regiment (Regular & TA) is generally a wheeled organisation that might be expected to have 2 Field Squadrons, a Support Squadron and possibly an Airfield Damage Repair (ADR) Squadron. Engineer regiments supporting 3(UK) Division could be structured along the lines of the Armoured Divisional Engineer Regiment.

Combat Engineer Tractor

(141 in service) Weight 17,010kg: Length 7.54m: Height 2.67m: Road Speed 56kph: Road Range 480kms: Fuel Capacity 430 litres: Engine Rolls-Royce C6TCR: Engine Power 320bhp: Crew 2: Armament 1 x 7.62 machine gun.

First seen in service in 1977 the Combat Engineer Tractor (CET) is a versatile tracked AFV that can clear obstacles, dig pits, prepare barriers and tow other vehicles out of impossible positions. In short it is an engineer vehicle that can assist in almost every battlefield task and has an impressive amphibious capability. The 100m winch cable can be fired from the CET by rocket, and using an anchor, can assist in dragging the vehicle up steep slopes and over river banks. CET is found mainly in the Div Engr Regts and the UK Engr Regts. India has 39 x CET in service and Singapore is believed to have another 18.

Replacement plans for the CET are already underway and during 1995 it is believed that the UK MOD will initiate a feasibility study for the next generation Armoured Combat Engineer Vehicle. The new vehicle will be called "Terrier" and indications are that some 100 vehicles could be required from 2005.

Chieftain Assault Vehicle Royal Engineers - CHAVRE

The CHAVRE has a crew of 4, and the Chieftain gun turret has been removed and replaced by an armoured "penthouse" upon which the commanders cupola is situated. Mounted over the vehicle structure are three "hampers" one at the front of the vehicle and two at the rear. These "hampers" carry engineer stores such as trackway, facines or general equipment. A typical "hamper" load could be 4 x rolls of Class 60 trackway or 3 x fascines.

At the front of the vehicle is a dozer blade or mine plough (either can be used) and at the rear there is a hydraulic winch capable of pulling 10 tons. In the centre of the vehicle is a crane capable of lifting 3.5 tons and with a telescopic jib that extends to 5 metres. A giant viper can be towed and the vehicle carries a 7.62mm machine gun for local defence.

The MOD has ordered 48 vehicles of which some 35 had been delivered at the end of 1994. We would expect all 48 vehicles to be in service by the end of 1995. CHAVRE replaces the Centurion Mk 5 Assault Vehicle Royal Engineers that had been in service since the early 1960s.

Chieftain Bridgelayer (AVLB)

(48 in service) Weight 53,300kg: Length 13.74m: Height 3.92m: Width 4.16m: Max Road Speed 42kph: Road Range 400km: Engine L60 No4 Mark 7A: Engine Power 730bhp: Fuel Capacity 886 litres: Bridge Length (No. 8 Bridge) 24,38m: Bridge Width (No 8 Bridge) 4.16m: Bridge Weight (No 8 Bridge) 12,200kg: Crew 3: Armament 2 x 7.62mm machine guns.

In service since l974 the Chieftain AVLB can carry the No 8 Bridge (24m long) and the No 9 Bridge (l3m long). The normal times taken to lay a No 8 Bridge across a 24m gap is about 5 minutes and the bridge can be recovered from the far side of the gap, and carried along behind the battlegroup being supported. The AVLB is to be found mainly in 32 Engineer Regiment in Germany with smaller numbers in the UK.

M2/3 Bridge

Weight 22,000kg: Length 11.3m: Height 3.58m: Width 2.99m: Width (bridge deployed) 1416mm: Max Road Speed 60kph: Water Speed 15kph: Road Range 1,000kms: Crew 4.

There are approximately 72 x M2 vehicles in British Army service and they are to be found mainly in 28 Engr Regt in Germany and a TA Regt in the UK. The M2 can be driven into a river and used as a ferry, or when bolted together form a bridge capable of taking vehicles as heavy as the Challenger MBT. The M2 is a German vehicle which first entered service in 1972.

We expect the M2 Bridge to be replaced by the M3 Bridge during 1996/97. The M3 has three bridging ramps in place of the four on the M2, a length increase of 2.3 metres, increased buoyancy and can be driven in the water from both ends. The vehicle is powered by marine jets instead of propellers and only 2 x ferries are required to ferry an MBT instead of the 5 x M2's needed for the same task. We believe that the British Army intends to purchase some 50 of these vehicles and that the current cost is in the region of £1 million per vehicle.

During 1994 3 x M3 bridges were being extensively trialled by the British Army.

Medium Girder Bridge (MGB)

The MGB is a simple system of lightweight components that can be easily manhandled to construct a bridge capable of taking the heaviest AFVs. Two MGBs are held by the bridging troop in the support squadron of a divisional engineer regiment.

Single span bridge - 30m long which can be built by about 25 men in 45 minutes.

Multi span bridge - a combination of 26.5m spans. Therefore a 2 span bridge will cross a 51m gap and a 3 span bridge a 76m gap. If necessary the MGB pontoons can be joined together to form a ferry.
During late 1994 a team from 35 Engr Regt set a new world record by building a single storey 9 metre bridge in 10 mins and 34 secs. By 1995 the manufacturer Williams Fairey claimed that the MGB was in service with some 35 nations world wide. MGB is due to be replaced by the BR90 system (although some MGB will be retained for certain operational requirements).

Class 16 Airportable Bridge

A much lighter bridge than the MGB the Class 16 can be carried assembled under a Chinook helicopter or in 3 x 3/4 ton vehicles with trailers. A 15m bridge can be constructed by 15 men in 20 minutes. The Class 16 can also be made into a ferry which is capable of carrying the heaviest AFVs.

Giant Viper

Trailer Weight 2136 kgs; Hose Length 230m; Cleared Zone 180m x 7.5m wide.

The Giant Viper is a system which is used for clearing lanes through a minefield. It consists of a hose which is filled with explosive, and this hose is carried in a special trailer which is fitted with a rocket. The trailer, containing rocket and hose is towed behind vehicles such as the CHAVRE, CET or Fv 432.

The trailer is positioned 150m from the edge of the minefield and when the rocket is fired, the explosive filled hose is carried into the minefield. The subsequent explosion of the hose will clear a lane 180m long and 7.5m wide and trials analysis suggest that in a "cleared" lane over 90% of anti tank mines will have been neutralised.

Bar Mine (Anti-Tank)

Weight 11kg: Length 1.2m: Width 0.1m: Explosive Weight 8.4kg.

The Bar Mine is usually mechanically laid by a plough type vehicle that can be towed behind an AFV 432 or Warrior. The Bar Mines can be placed on a conveyer inside the APC from where they are fed into the layer, which then deposits them in the furrow automatically covering them with soil. Up to 600 mines can be laid in one hour by one vehicle with a 3-man crew.

Ranger Mine (Anti-Personnel)

The Ranger Mine is an anti-personnel device which is launched from a projector carried on the roof of an AFV 432. This projector can carry 72 tubes and each of these tubes can hold up to 18 mines. When the tube is fired the mines are projected in a random pattern out to a distance of 100m. Each mine carries a 10gm charge of PDX and these charges are capable of causing serious injury to personnel who trip them. The mine is of plastic construction and difficult to detect using conventional equipment.

Claymore Mine (Anti-Personnel)

Weight 1,58kg: Length 021m: Width 0.03m: Charge Weight 0.68kg.

The Claymore Mine comes in a small crescent shaped container which sits on a pair of bipod legs. The mine is positioned facing the enemy and fired by remote control from distances up to 300m away. On firing, the mine throws about 700 ball-bearings out to a range of about 50m on a 60deg. arc. First purchased from the US in 1963, the Claymore is a superb anti-infantry weapon that will probably be in service for many years to come.

Horizontal Action Mine (Anti-Tank)

Length 0.26m: Weight 12kg: Diameter 0.2m: Range 75m.

This French mine is used on route armour ambushes. The mine is placed at the side of the road and a trip wire is strung out across the vehicle path. When the vehicle trips the wire a shaped charge from the mine is fired into the side of the vehicle.

Mark 7 Mine (Anti-Tank)

Charge Weight 8.89kg: Mine Weight 13.6kg: Diameter 0.13m.

The Mark 7 Mine has been in service for many years and when stocks are exhausted will be replaced by the Bar Mine.

Mine Detectors

No 4C

Weight 9.15kg: Detection Depth (soil) 0.51m.

The No 4C is the standard mine detector and has been in service since 1968.
The No 4C is a lightweight system that can detect mines down to a depth of 51m and an engineer field troop using these detectors can clear an 8m lane in a minefield 100m deep, in about 4-5 hours.
During the Gulf War a "one off purchase" of approximately 200 x AN-19 mine detectors (manufacturers Nobel-Tech) was made to provide a mine detector capable of dealing effectively with local conditions. These mine detectors have not been issued for general service and the current UK MOD evaluation of a number of different systems designed to replace the No 4C continues. Current estimates are that some 1000 new mine detectors will be required and that a decision is expected regarding the replacement detector during mid 1995.

Minefields laid by the REs will usually be a mix of Bar (anti-tank) and Ranger (anti-personnel) mines with a liberal sprinkling of anti-handling devices. Minefields will always be covered by artillery and mortar fire to make mine clearance operations by the enemy difficult, with ATGWs usually sited in positions covering the minefield that will give them flank shoots onto enemy mineploughs that might spearhead a minefield crossing operation.

Mines in the New Century

Studies are currently underway to identify the type of anti-personnel and anti-tank mines that will be in service with the British Army during the early part of the next century. The mines that finally come into service will almost certainly have a scatterable capability from either armoured vehicles or helicopters and contain some form of intelligent reaction. They will probably be capable of remote arming on an on/off basis with a self destruct capability. Sensors that can differentiate between different targets will almost certainly be considered and an anti-helicopter capability will probably be considered as essential.

These intelligent mines will probably resemble the US FASCAM (Family of Scatterable Mines) System. The FASCAM system is composed of a family of mines based upon a set of common components. Mines in the family include:

Area Denial Artillery Munition (ADAM) - Artillery Delivered
Remote Anti-Armour Mine (RAAM) - Artillery Delivered
Ground Emplaced Mine Scattering System (GEMSS) - Ground Launcher Delivered
Modular Pack Mine System (MOPMS) - 2 or 4 Man Hand Carry
Gator Anti Armour System - Aircraft Delivered
Volcano Anti Tank and Anti-personnel System - Ground/Helicopter Delivery
Wide Area Mine (WAM) - Hand emplaced/Ground Launched/Helicopter Launched
Pursuit Deterrent Munition (PDM) - Hand Emplaced Munition*.

* Believed to be in service with UK Special Forces.

There has been much recent speculation regarding an international ban on the use of anti-personnel mines. The daily loss of life in many areas of the world due to mines from previous conflicts killing and maiming civilians is a disgrace and a subject that needs urgent attention. In our opinion a simple ban on mines would be totally ineffective. There is no means of policing this type of ban and anti-personnel mines are such an important battlefield asset that most countries will continue to manufacture them, with their consequent sale in the world market inevitable.

A far better suggestion and one that would cut civilian casualty rates by at least 90% would be for anti-personnel mines to be manufactured with an electronic self destruct device linked to a battery. When the battery was completely discharged (possibly after 8 weeks) the mine would self destruct. Such a system is almost foolproof and the majority of anti-personnel mines would self destruct before civilians return to their homes.

BR90 Family of Bridges

In early 1994 the UK MOD announced that the production order had been placed for the BR90 family of bridges that are planned to enter service between January 1996 and June 1997 as follows:

January 1996	- General Support Bridge
November 1996	- Close Support Bridge
May 1997	- Two Span Bridge
June 1997	- Long Span Bridge

BR90 will be deployed with Royal Engineer units in both Germany and the United Kingdom. The production order was issued and accepted in October 1993 and the value of the order is approximately £140 million. This order will secure up to 250 jobs at the prime contractor, Thompson Defence Projects in Wolverhampton, as well as 50 jobs at Unipower in Watford plus many other sub-contractors.

The components of the system are:

Close Support Bridge - This consists of three tank launched bridges capable of being carried on the in-service Chieftain bridgelayer and a TBT (Tank Bridge Transporter) truck.

	Weight	Length	Gap
No 10 Bridge	13 tons	26m	24.5m
No 11 Bridge	7.4 tons	16m	14.5m
No 12 Bridge	5.3 tons	13.5m	12m

The existing No 8 and No 9 bridges carried in the Chieftain AVLB will be retained in service.

The Unipower TBT 8 x 8 truck can carry 1 x No 1 Bridge, 1 x No 11 Bridge or 2 x No 12 Bridges. The TBT has an unladen weight of 21 tons and is also used to transport the General Support Bridge.

General Support Bridge - This system utilises the Automotive Bridge Launching Equipment (ABLE) that is capable of launching bridges up to 44 metres in length. The ABLE vehicle is positioned with its rear pointing across the gap to be crossed and a lightweight launch rail extended across the gap.
The bridge is then assembled and winched across the gap supported by the rail, with sections added until the gap is crossed. Once the bridge has crossed the gap the ABLE launch rail is recovered. A standard ABLE system set consists of an ABLE vehicle and 2 x TBT carrying a 32 metre bridge set.

It is believed that a 32m bridge can be built by 10 men in about 25 minutes.

Spanning Systems - There are two basic spanning systems. The long span systems allows for lengthening a 32 metre span to 44 metres using ABLE, and the two span system allows 2 x 32 metre bridge sets to be constructed by ABLE and secured in the middle by piers or floating pontoons, crossing a total gap of about 60 metres.

CHAPTER 9 - COMMUNICATIONS

"Use of a radio set should be considered high treason".

German Staff Officer following the Battle of Tannenburg in August 1914. The Russians broadcast their battle orders in clear and the Germans had prior knowledge of every Russian move. The Russian Army suffered a devastating defeat.

"The guys in signals intelligence knew exactly what Saddam Hussein was going to do and how he was going to do it - the problem is that the guys in the State Department didn't want to believe them".

Former CIA Officer - BBC Radio 4 - 14 March 1995

The Royal Corps of Signals

The Royal Corps of Signals (R Signals) provide the communications throughout the command system of the Army. Individual battlegroups are responsible for their own internal communications, but all communications from Brigade level and above are the responsibility of the Royal Signals.

Information is the lifeblood of any military formation in battle and it is the responsibility of the Royal Signals to ensure the speedy and accurate passage of information that enables commanders to make informed and timely decisions, and to ensure that those decisions are passed to the fighting troops in contact with the enemy. The rapid, accurate and secure employment of command, control and communications systems maximises the effect of the military force available and consequently the Royal Signals act as an extremely significant 'Force Multiplier'.

The Royal Corps of Signals provides about 9% of the Army's manpower with 11 Regular and 11 Territorial Army Regiments, each generally consisting of between 3 and up to 6 Sqns with between 400 and 1,000 personnel. In addition, there are 20 Regular and 2 Territorial Army Independent Squadrons, each of which has about 200 men, and 4 Independent Signal Troops of between 10 and 80 men each. Royal Signals personnel are found wherever the Army is deployed including every UK and NATO headquarters in the world. The Headquarters of the Corps is at the Royal School of Signals (RSS) located at Blandford in Dorset.

Royal Signals units based in the United Kingdom provide command and control communications for forces that have operational roles both in the UK itself, including Northern Ireland, and overseas including mainland Western Europe and further afield wherever the Army finds itself. There are a number of Royal Signals units permanently based in Germany, Holland and Belgium from where they provide the necessary command and control communications and Electronic

Warfare (EW) support for both the British Army and other NATO forces based in Europe.

Royal Signals units are also based in Cyprus, Hong Kong, the Falkland Islands, Belize and Gibraltar. Regular Army Royal Signals units based in the United Kingdom in support of NATO include:

UK Units - Providing NATO Support

2 Signal Regiment which provides command and Control communications for up to three Divisions in the ARRC including one multi-national Division.

3 (UK) Mechanised Division Headquarters and Signal Regiment. This Regiment provides the command and control communications for 3 (UK) Division that deploys to Germany as part of the Allied Command Europe (ACE) Rapid Reaction Corps.

1(Mechanised) Brigade Signal Squadron. This unit provides communications for the UK Mobile Force (Land) which deploys to Northern Germany and Denmark.

209 Signal Squadron supports 19 (Mechanised) Brigade based in Catterick which is part of the ARRC.

210 (Airmobile) Brigade Signal Squadron provides communications for 24 (Airmobile) Brigade based in Colchester.

216 Parachute Signal Squadron is part of 5th Airborne Brigade which is able to operate either in the UK, within the NATO area of operations or worldwide.

249 (AMF(L)) Signal Squadron provides communications for a multi-national NATO Brigade that deploys to Norway and Denmark or Turkey and Greece.

264 (SAS) Signal Squadron supports the Special Air Service Regiment.

(UK Units - Supporting National Defence Formations)

Regular Army Royal Signals units based in the UK which are not allocated to NATO include:

11 Signal Regiment stationed at Blandford in Dorset is the administrative unit for the Royal School of Signals (RSS) and carries out basic Trade Training, promotion courses for potential Non Commissioned Officers and basic training for the TA soldiers of the Royal Signals.

15 Signal Regiment provides command and control communications for the security forces in Northern Ireland. This Regiment has 3 Squadrons to support the

3 Brigades in the Province.

30 Signal Regiment which provides communications for all Army and RAF forces that deploy outside the NATO area of operations. This Regiment always maintains troops who are held on 24 hours notice to move to anywhere in the world. One Squadron of the Queen's Gurkha Signal Regiment is permanently attached to 30 Signal Regiment and serves in the United Kingdom.

Units Deployed Outside the UK

Royal Signals units that are permanently deployed in Europe in support of British and other NATO forces include:

1 (UK) Armoured Division Headquarters and Signal Regiment. This Regiment which has three Armoured Brigade Squadrons provides communications for the Divisional Headquarters and the three Brigades in the 1st (UK) Armoured Division.

7 (ARRC) Signal Regiment provides command and control communications for the ARRC headquarters which involves providing communications to the formation's multi-national Divisions.

14 Signal Regiment (Electronic Warfare) provides the highly sophisticated electronic warfare support for the Headquarters of the ARRC and for the 1st and 3rd (UK) Divisions. In late 1995 14 Sig Regiment will return to the UK where it will be stationed at the former RAF base at Brawdy in Wales.

16 Signal Regiment. This Regiment provides communication support for a number of multi-national logistic organisations and fixed communications for British Forces Germany and RAF Germany.

A Royal Signals Regiment is based in Cyprus to support the Army and RAF forces in the Sovereign Base Areas and a Royal Signals Squadron supports the United Nations Force. In Hong Kong the Queen's Gurkha Signals Regiment supports the Gurkha Field Force and provides the command and control communication system for the forces in the colony as a whole. Current plans are for the Queen's Gurkha Signals to be reduced to Squadron strength before 1997.

(TA Units - At 1 Mar 1995)
Royal Signals Territorial Army (TA) units include:

11 (ARRC) Signal Brigade based in Liverpool comprises the following units that all deploy to mainland Europe to provide communications for various headquarters in the ARRC.

33rd (Lancashire and Cheshire)Signal Regiment (V) based in Liverpool.

34th (Northern) Signal Regiment (V) based in Middlesbrough.
35th (South Midland) Signal Regiment (V) based in Birmingham.
36th (Eastern)Signal Regiment (V) based in London 55th Signal Regiment (V) based in Liverpool.

The Regular Army's 2 Signal Regiment also comes under the command of 11 Signal Brigade.

2nd (National Communications) Signal Brigade with its headquarters in Corsham is responsible for providing communication for Military Home Defence and operates the Army Fixed Telecommunications System (AFTS). Units include:

31 (Special Task) Signal Regiment(V) based in London.
32 (Scottish) Signal Regiment(V) based in Glasgow.
37 (Wessex and Welsh) Signal Regiment(V) based in Redditch.
38 Signal Regiment(V) based in Sheffield.
71 (Yeomanry) Signal Regiment(V) based in Bexleyheath.
56 Signal Squadron(V) based in Reading.

63 (V) SAS Signal Squadron is an independent unit that provides communication support for the Territorial Army Special Air Service Regiments.

TA Organisation - Future Changes

The first indications as to how the latest TA reorganisations will affect the Royal Signals are as follows:

3 x Ptarmigan Regiments
2 x Euromux Regiments
6 x National Communications Regiments
3 x Independent Signals Squadrons
2 x Special Communications Squadrons
The 2 (National Communications) Brigade units will be restructured to provide Regional and National Communications support to Land Command. An independent Combat Service Support Group Squadron will also be formed.

Armoured Divisional Signal Regiment Organisation

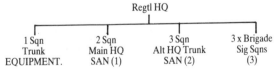

Notes: (1) SAN - Secondary Access Node (2) A Divisional HQ will have two HQs to allow for movement and possible destruction. The main HQ will be set up for approx 24 hrs with the alternate HQ (Alt HQ) set up 20-30 kms away on the proposed line of march of the division. When the Main HQ closes to move to a new location the Alt HQ becomes the Main HQ for another 24 hour period. (3) Expect a Brigade Sig Sqn to have a Radio Troop and a SAN Troop.

R Signals units are currently operating the following types of major equipment:

> Mobile Satellite Terminals
> HF, VHF and UHF Radios
> Radio Relay (carrying telephone & teleprinter links)
> Teleprinters, Fax, CCTV and ADP Equipment
> Computers
> Line

The communications systems used by the Royal Signals include:

Ptarmigan

Ptarmigan is a mobile, secure battlefield system that incorporates the latest technology and has been designed to improve communications reliability, capacity and interoperability.

Built by Siemens-Plessey Christchurch in the mid 1980s Ptarmigan is a user-friendly, computer controlled communications system which was initially designed to meet the needs of the British Army in Germany. The system consists of a network of electronic exchanges or Trunk Switches that are connected by satellite and multichannel radio relay (TRIFFID) links that provide voice, data, telegraph and fax communications. The Trunk Switch, radio and satellite relays together with their support vehicles comprise a 'Trunk Node' and all field headquarters include a group of communications vehicles that contain an Access Switch which can be connected to any Trunk Switch giving access to the system. This ensures that headquarters have exceptional flexibility in siting and trunk communications then present no constraints on operations.

Additionally Ptarmigan has a mobile telephone or Single Channel Radio Access (SCRA) which gives isolated or mobile users an entry point into the entire system.

Triffid

Radio relay links within Ptarmigan are provided by TRIFFID which is a radio equipment that has 3 interchangeable radio frequency modules known as 'heads'. Each TRIFFID link carries the equivalent of up to 32 voice circuits at a data rate of 512 kb/s plus an engineering circuit.

118

Euromux

EUROMUX is a trunk system manufactured by Racal which is similar in principle to the PTARMIGAN system and is interoperable with the trunk systems of other NATO armies. TRIFFID is used to provide the relay links within the system.

Clansman

Is the name given to the in-service family of tactical radios with which the British Army is currently equipped to provide communications from formation headquarters forward to the fighting units. CLANSMAN is a lighter, far more reliable and adaptable system than the ageing LARKSPUR system that it replaced during the early 1980s. In its turn CLANSMAN will be replaced by BOWMAN.

Clansman Manpack Radios

Used By Weight Range Freq coverage

PRC 349 Inf Sec 1.5 kg 2km 37-46.975
PRC 350 Inf Pl or Sec 3.6 kg 5km 36-56.975
PRC 351 Coy/Sqn 6.3 kg 8km 30-75.975
PRC 352 Coy/Sqn 9.2 kg 16km 30-75.975 PRC 320 Coy/Pl ll kg 50km 2-29.999

Clansman Vehicle Radios

	Used By	Weight	Range	Freq coverage
VRC 321	Command Nets	23 kg	60km	1.5-29.999
VRC-322	Command Nets	52 kg	80km	1.5-29.999
VRC-353	Bn/Coy/Sqn	22 kg	30km	30-75.975

On the FEBA these Clansman radios are operated by the Battlegroup Signal Platoons but further back (generally Brigade level and backwards towards Divisional, Corps and Army HQ) will be the responsibility of the Royal Signals.

Bowman

Bowman is a tactical communications system that has been designed to provide a replacement for the series of Clansman radios currently in service with the British Army. Bowman will almost certainly make use of the latest packet radio technology and a contract for a 25 station demonstrator system was awarded to Racal-BCC in 1988.

The project demonstration phase is now underway with an expected production contract worth one £1.9 billion to be awarded in May 1996.
There appear to be three serious contenders for the contract:-

GEC/Marconi/Thomson-CSF	-	Arrowhead System
Siemens Plessey/Racal Radio	-	Yeoman System
ITT/BAe/Hunting/N Telecom	-	Crossbow System

The Bowman project will probably finally dovetail with a number of major European communications requirements and it would not be a great surprise if the final outcome of the Bowman project is a Euro-equipment with sales being made to several European nations, and manufacture being handled by a Euro-consortium. The latest statement (Feb 95) from the MOD suggests that Bowman will be in service "by January 2000".

Satellite Communications (SATCOM)

The Royal Signals deploys transportable and manpack satellite ground stations to provide communications links for headquarters or small groups located in remote parts of the world via its SKYNET 4B system. Operations in the Falklands and Namibia proved the value of satellite communications and during the Gulf war there was an extensive use of SATCOM ground terminals particularly the Racal VSC501. It is expected that a new series of SKYNET 5 satellites will be introduced to enhance SATCOM facilities in the future.

Wavell

Wavell is a battlefield automatic data processing computer system, designed to accept information from all the battlefield intelligence agencies, and produce this information on request in hard copy or on a VDU. Information is then used to assist commanders and their staff with the analysis of intelligence and subsequent conduct of operations. Each headquarters from Corps down to Brigade level is equipped with its own Wavell computers that are linked to the PTARMIGAN system

Wavell will almost certainly be continually upgraded during the 1990s with interfaces planned for operation with BATES, ADCIS (Air Defence Command Information System) and Vixen. The integration of Wavell with the German HEROS, French SACRA and US MCS Command and Control system will probably be a high priority.

Slim

SLIM is a new system using the personal computer equipment used in the Gulf war which is being developed to complement WAVELL.

Bates

BATES is a battlefield artillery engagement system which has been designed to centralise the command and control of artillery, with all fire missions being routed through a central contol cell and then passed on to the appropriate fire units. Access to the system is available down to the level of artillery FOOs (Forward Observation Officers) who have their own digital entry devices. BATES will eventually replace FACE (Forward Artillery Computing Equipment).

Artillery intelligence entered in the system is available for commanders and their staff through the Wavell interface and much of the routine and logistic tasks are processed by the equipment, thus freeing the staff for other tasks.

BATES is an important part of the MLRS - AS 90 - PHOENIX - COBRA series of battlefield fire support systems and when it is finally in service will provide valuable support to these equipments. However, there appear to have been serious delays in bringing BATES into service, and once in service there could be significant teething problems as BATES is integrated with other systems.

We believe that some £50 million has been spent on BATES and that there will eventually be up to 200 systems in operation with the British Army.

Vixen

Vixen has been designed to provide an automated system for processing of electronic intelligence. It will probably be mounted in soft skinned vehicles and deployed with the electronic warfare regiment which amongst its many tasks listens to enemy signal traffic and passes vital intelligence to the operational staff. Vixen became operational in late 1992 and it is probable that the system is linked to the existing electronic direction finding equipment subsequently feeding results into the BATES and Wavell ADP systems. The cost of the Vixen system was believed to be in the region of £36.5 million.

Scimitar

Scimitar has been designed to provide a secure combat net communications system to include a frequency agile ability for use in areas where the ECM threat is high. Equipments are man portable or vehicle mounted and the system has three basic equipments:

Scimitar H (HF radio)
Freq 1.6 - 30MHz - 284000 channels - Weight 4.0 kgs (manpack).
Scimitar V (VHF vehicle or man-pack radio)
Freq 30-88MHz - 2320 channels - Weight 4.8 kgs (manpack)
Scimitar M (Pocket sized VHF radio)
Freq 68 - 88MHz - 800 channels - Weight 0.5 kg.

Scimitar is believed to be in use with the British Army and is known to be in use with Jordan, Portugal, Turkey and Sweden. Manufactured by Plessey the average cost of a Scimitar radio is probably in the area of 8,000 pounds.

Jaguar

Jaguar is manufactured by Racal Tacticom and is a similar system to Scimitar with the ability to frequency hop in ECM environments. The radio can be used in both the vehicle and manpack roles and the main characteristics are as follows:

Frequency Range	30-88MHz
Temperature Range	-40 to 70 degrees C
Weight	5 kgs
Channels	2320
Spacing	25 kHz

Jaguar is in service with the British Army and US Navy. Over 30 nations are currently using this equipment and sales to date are believed to be in excess of £120 million.

Army Fixed Telecommunications Systems

The peacetime management of the Army depends heavily on effective communications . The Royal Signals Army Fixed Telecommunication System (AFTS) provides all the telephone, telegraph, facsimile, data systems and radio and line links for the Army in the United Kingdom. AFTS is operated and maintained by 2 (National Communications) Brigade and the system serves over 40,000 subscribers. The staff required to operate the AFTS is approximately 1,100 of whom 40% are military personnel who are located all over the UK in six (Fixed Service) Signal Squadrons supported by operational, engineering, planning and co-ordination staff at Headquarters 2 (NC) Brigade at Corsham in Wiltshire.

One of the ADP systems in the UKLF system is MAPPER which stands for Maintenance, Preparation and Presentation of Executive Reports. This system is used both as a peacetime management aid to staffs in major headquarters but also for command and control of Military Home Defence and was expanded for use in the Gulf war when MAPPER stations were deployed to Saudi Arabia and linked back to the United Kingdom. Its success in the Gulf has led to the system being used in post Gulf war operations including the Balkans.

In Germany the Telecommunications Group Headquarters based at Rheindahlen provides a sophisticated fixed communications system based on the Integrated Services Digital Network (ISDN). Project Rodin which is intended to modernise the fixed communications system for both the Army and the RAF in Germany will, when introduced, use state of the art digital technology and will be able to interact with other German and British military and civilian networks.

The Communications Projects Division (CPD) provides engineering support for military fixed communications systems worldwide. CPD is part of the Royal School of Signals at Blandford in Dorset.

CHAPTER 10 - COMBAT SERVICE SUPPORT

"Give them great meals of beef and iron and steel, they will eat like wolves and fight like devils".

King Henry V Act III - William Shakespeare.

"It is more important to destroy those places that contain the elements of military power (the magazines and stores) than soldiers, who are nothing without their stores."

Systeme de Guerre moderne - General Comte de Cessac 1797

Logistic Support

Following the 1990 Logistic Support Review the British Army has decided that in the future logistic support will be based upon the twin pillars of service support (the supply chain) and equipment support (the maintenance of equipment).

Combat Service Support within the British Army is now provided by the Royal Logistic Corps (RLC), the Royal Electrical and Mechanical Engineers (REME) and the Royal Army Medical Corps (RAMC).

Within any fighting formation logistic units from these Corps typically represent about 30% of the manpower total of an Armoured Division, and with the exception of certain members of the RAMC all are fully trained fighting soldiers.

The task of the logistic units on operations is to maintain the combat units in the field which entails:

a. SUPPLY AND DISTRIBUTION - of ammunition, fuel, lubricants, rations and spare parts.

b. RECOVERY AND REPAIR - of battle damaged and unserviceable equipment.

c. TREATMENT AND EVACUATION - of casualties.

In a Division the commanders of the logistic units all operate from a separate, self contained headquarters under the command of a Colonel who holds the appointment of the Division's Deputy Chief of Staff (DCOS). This headquarters, usually known as the Divisional Headquarters (Rear), co-ordinates the whole of the logistic support of the Division in battle.

Supplies, reinforcements and returning casualties pass through an area located to the rear of the Division where some of the less mobile logistic units are located. This area is known as the Divisional Admin Area (DAA) and its staff is responsible for co-ordinating the flow of all material and personnel into and out of the Divisional area.

The Royal Logistic Corps (RLC)

The RLC is the youngest Corps in the Army and was formed in April 1993 as a result of the recommendations of the Logistic Support Review. The RLC results from the amalgamation of the Royal Corps of Transport (RCT), the Royal Army Ordnance Corps (RAOC), the Army Catering Corps (ACC), the Royal Pioneer Corps (RPC) and elements of the Royal Enginers (RE). The Corps makes up about 16% of the Army with 20,000 Regular soldiers and 10,000 Territorial Army soldiers wearing its cap badge.

The RLC has very broad responsibilities throughout the Army including the movement of personnel throughout the world, the Army's air dispatch service, maritime and rail transport, operational resupply, explosive ordnance disposal which includes the hazardous bomb disposal duties in Northern Ireland and in mainland Britain, the operation of numerous very large vehicle and stores depots both in the UK and overseas, the training and provision of cooks to virtually all units in the Army, the provision of pioneer labour and the Army's postal and courier service.

The principle field elements of the RLC are the Close Support and the General Support Regiments whose primary role is to supply the fighting units with ammunition, fuel and rations (Combat Supplies).

A division has an integral Close Support Regiment which is responsible for manning and operating the supply chain to Brigades and Divisional units.

Close Support Regiment RLC

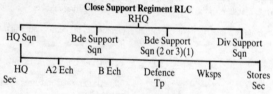

Note:
(1) A regiment could have two or three brigade support sqns depending upon the size of the division being supported. (2) Some of these regiments may have a Postal and Courier Sqn.

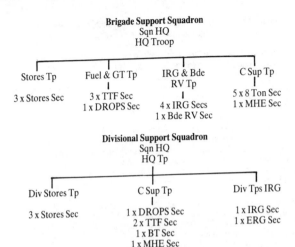

Brigade Support Squadron
Sqn HQ
HQ Troop

Stores Tp	Fuel & GT Tp	IRG & Bde RV Tp	C Sup Tp
3 x Stores Sec	3 x TTF Sec 1 x DROPS Sec	4 x IRG Secs 1 x Bde RV Sec	5 x 8 Ton Sec 1 x MHE Sec

Divisional Support Squadron
Sqn HQ
HQ Tp

Div Stores Tp	C Sup Tp	Div Tps IRG
3 x Stores Sec	1 x DROPS Sec 2 x TTF Sec 1 x BT Sec 1 x MHE Sec	1 x IRG Sec 1 x ERG Sec

The General Support Regiment's role is primarily to supply ammunition to the Royal Artillery using DROPS vehicles and to provide Tank Transporters that move armoured vehicles more rapidly and economically than moving them on their own tracks.

General Support Regiment RLC

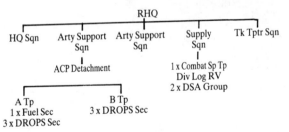

RHQ

HQ Sqn	Arty Support Sqn	Arty Support Sqn	Supply Sqn	Tk Tptr Sqn
	ACP Detachment		1 x Combat Sp Tp Div Log RV 2 x DSA Group	

A Tp 1 x Fuel Sec 3 x DROPS Sec	B Tp 3 x DROPS Sec

Both types of Regiment have large sections holding stores both on wheels and on the ground.

A Division will typically require about 1,000 tons of Combat Supplies a day but demand can easily exceed that amount in high intensity operations.

Battlegroups in contact with the enemy can carry a limited amount of C Sups, particularly ammunition, with them which is replenished from RLC vehicles located immediately to the rear of battlegroups in Immediate Replenishment Groups (IRGs). As the IRG vehicles are emptied they return to the RLC Squadron location and fully loaded replacements are automatically sent forward so that a constant supply is always available to the battlegroup.

Ammunition and spares are generally carried on NATO standard pallets which are loaded to meet the anticipated requirements of particular units and if required bulk is broken at the IRG location. Fuel is usually carried in bulk fuel tankers (TTFs) which top-up battlegroup vehicles direct. However there is still a requirement for a large number of the traditional jerricans. Much of the other fuel is delivered to the forward areas through the NATO Central European Pipeline System (CEPS).

Artillery ammunition constitutes by far the largest single element in the logistic pipeline and the bulk of it is delivered directly to the Royal Artillery guns, rocket and missile launchers by RLC Demountable Rack Offloading and Pickup System (DROPS) vehicles from the General Support Regiment, which are capable of meeting the requirement of even the highest intensity consumption.

RLC Miscellaneous
Apart from the RLC units that provide direct support the operational formations the RLC is directly responsible for are:

Army School of Mechanical Transport - Leconfield
Base Ordnance Depots (Bicester & Donnington)
Base Ammunition Depots (Longtown & Kineton)
Army School of Ammunition (Temple Herdwyke)
Petroleum Centre (West Moors)
Army Base Vehicle Organisation (Ashchurch)
Armoured Vehicle Sub Depot (Ludgershall)
Army School of Catering (Aldershot)
Royal Logistic Corps Training Centre (Deepcut)

At the end of January 1995 the MOD had 245,609 vehicles on charge (both operational and administrative) with the individual service allocation as follows:

Royal Navy	-	6,555
Royal Air Force	-	151,816
Army	-	87,238

Of the Army's vehicle total, during February 1995 the Land Rover fleet was comprised of the following:

Truck Utility Light (TUL)	- 4,584
Truck Utility Medium (TUM)	- 10,824
1 Tonne	- 750

Daily Messing Rates

The allowances per day for catering purposes are based on a ration scale costed at current prices and known as the daily messing rate (DMR). The ration scale is the same for all three services, and contrary to popular army belief the RAF is not supplied with wine etc at public expense. The rate per day is the amount that the catering organisation has to feed each individual serviceman or servicewoman.

The scale is costed to the supply source of the food items. When the source of supply is more expensive due to local conditions the DMR is set higher to take account of local costs. A general overseas ration scale exists for overseas bases and attachments. This scale has a higher calorific value to take into account the conditions of heat, cold or humidity that can be encountered.

The UK ration scale is designed to provide 2,900 kilo calories nett- that is after loss through preparation and cooking. The general overseas ration scale includes an arduous duty allowance to allow for climate and provides some 3,400 kilo-calories nett. In field conditions where personel are fed from operational ration packs 3,800 kilo calories are provided.

RLC Catering Units feed the Army, generally using detachments of cooks attached to units. The following were the daily messing rates (DMR) at the end of 1994:

Army, RAF and RN Shore Establishments	£1.75 per day
RN Ships and Submarines	£1.86 per day
Falkland Islands	£2.03 per day
Cyprus	£1.93 per day
Gibraltar	£2.07 per day

Postal & Courier

RLC units are also responsible for Army Postal & Courier Services. Army figures are impossible to identify but the numbers of items moved by the Defence Postal Services in the past four years is:

1990-91	56,607,788
1991-92	56,082,586
1992-93	37,567,378
1993-94	31,125,393 (27 Oct 94)

The Central Army Post Office (APO) is located at Mill Hill in North London and there are individual British Forces Post Offices (BFPO) wherever British Forces are stationed.

The Royal Electrical & Mechanical Engineers - REME

"Another lean unwash'd artificer"

King John Act IV - William Shakespeare

The Logistic Support review of 1990 recommended that Equipment Support should remain separate from the other logistic pillar of Service Support and consequently the REME has retained not only its own identity but expanded its responsibilities. Equipment Support encompasses equipment management, engineering support, supply management, provisioning for vehicle and technical spares and financial management responsibilities for in-service equipment.

The aim of the REME is "To keep operationally fit equipment in the hands of the troops" and in the current financial environment it is important that this is carried out at the minimum possible cost. The equipment that REME is responsible for ranges from small arms and trucks to helicopters and Main Battle Tanks. All field force units have some integral REME support which will vary, depending on the size of the unit and the equipment held, from a few attached tradesmen up to a large Regimental Workshop of over 200 men.

In war REME is responsible for the recovery and repair of battle damaged and unserviceable equipments.

The development of highly technical weapon systems and other equipment has meant that REME has had to balance engineering and tactical considerations. On the one hand the increased scope for forward repair of equipment reduces the time out of action, but on the other hand engineering stability is required for the repair of complex systems. The major changes which have resulted from the Options for Change and Logistic Support Reviews are that four REME battalions have formed since 1993. One battalion is based in the United Kingdom to support 3(UK) Division and three battalions are based in Germany to support 1(UK) Armoured Division.

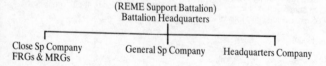

Note: Approx 450 personnel. At the beginning of 1995 there were 5 Regular REME Support battalions, 3 in Germany and 2 in the UK.

128

The Close Support Company will normally deploy a number of FRG's (Forward Repair Groups) and MRGs (Medium Repair Groups) in support of brigades. The company is mobile with armoured repair and recovery vehicles able to operate in the forward areas, carrying out forward repair of key nominated equipment often by the exchange of major assemblies. It is also capable of carrying out field repairs on priority equipment including telecommunications equipment and the repair of damage sustained by critical battle winning equipments.

The role of the General Support Company is to support the Close Support Companies and Divisional Troops. Tasks include the regeneration of fit power packs for use in forward repair and the repair of equipment backloaded from Close Support Companies. The General Support Company will normally be located to the rear of the divisional area in order to maximise productivity and minimise vulnerability.

In manpower terms the support available to 1(UK) Armoured Division in the ARRC will be somewhere in the area of the following:

Armoured Regiment	120
Armoured Recce Regiment	90
Armoured Infantry Battalion	90
Close Support Engineer Regiment	85
General Support Engineer Regiment	110
Field Regiment Royal Artillery	115
Air Defence Regiment Royal Artillery	160
Army Air Corps Regiment	130
Signals Regiment	60
RLC Close Support Regiment	75
RLC General Support Regiment	95
REME Battalion	450

Medical Services

"Stop dying at once and when you get up, get your bloody hair cut".

Colonel AD Wintle to Trooper Cedric Mayes (Royal Dragoons)
The patient lived for another 40 years.

The Royal Army Medical Corps (RAMC)

In peace, the personnel of the RAMC are based at the various medical installations throughout the world or in field force units and they are responsible for the health of the Army.

On operations, the RAMC is responsible for the care of the sick and wounded, with the subsequent evacuation of the wounded to hospitals in the rear areas. Each Brigade has a field ambulance which is a regular unit that operates in direct support of the battlegroups. These units are either armoured, airmobile or parachute trained. In addition each division has two field ambulance units that may be regular or TA that provide medical support for the divisional troops and can act as manoeuvre units for the forward brigades when required.

All field ambulance units have medical sections that consist of a medical officer and eight Combat Medical Technicians. These sub-units are located with the battlegroup or units being supported and they provide the necessary first line medical support. In addition, the field ambulance provides a dressing station where casualties are treated and may be resuscitated or stabilised before transfer to a field hospital. These units have the necessary integral ambulance support, both armoured and wheeled to transfer casualties from the first to second line medical units.

Field hospitals may be regular or TA and all are 200 bed facilities with a maximum of 8 surgical teams capable of carrying out life saving operations on some of the most difficult surgical cases. Since 1990 most regular medical units have been deployed on operations either in the Persian Gulf or the former Yugoslavia. Casualty Evacuation (CASEVAC) is by ambulance either armoured or wheeled and driven by RLC personnel or by helicopter when such aircraft are available. A Chinook helicopter is capable of carrying 44 stretcher cases and a Puma can carry 6 stretcher cases and 6 sitting cases.

The Queen Alexandra's Royal Army Nursing Corps (QARANC)

On the 1st April 1992 the QARANC became an all-nursing and totally professionally qualified Corps. Its male and female, officer and other rank personnel, provide the necessary qualified nursing support at all levels and covering a wide variety of nursing specialities. QARANC personnel can be found anywhere in the world where Army Medical services are required.

Royal Army Dental Corps (RADC)

The RADC is a professional corps that in late 1994 consisted over just over 400 officers and soldiers. The Corps fulfils the essential role of maintaining the dental health of the Army in peace and war, both at home and overseas. Qualified dentists and oral surgeons, hygienists, technicians and support ancillaries work in a wide variety of military units - from static and mobile dental clinics to field medical units, military hospitals and dental laboratories.

The Adjutant General's Corps (AGC)

The Adjutant General's Corps was formed on 1 April 1992 and its sole task is the management of the Army's most precious resource, its soldiers. The Corps absorbed the functions of six existing smaller corps; the Royal Military Police, the Royal Army Pay Corps, the Royal Army Educational Corps, the Royal Army

Chaplains Department, the Army Legal Corps and the Military Provost Staff Corps.

The Corps is organised into four branches, Staff and Personnel Support, Provost, Educational and Training Services and Army Legal Services. By 1995, after the incorporation of clerks from the remaining Arms, the AGC consisted of over 7,500 officers and soldiers.

AGC Miscellaneous

In addition to the AGC personnel attached to major units throughout the Army the Corps is directly responsible for the following:

AGC Depot and Training Centre (Worthy Down)
Directorate Staff & Personnel Support (Worthy Down)
Directorate Educational & Training Services (Worthy Down)
Provost Marshal (Army) (Worthy Down)
Army Pay Office (Ashton)
Army Finance & Audit Office (Ashton)
Command Pay Offices (Hong Kong & Cyprus)
Regimental Pay Offices (Glasgow, Chester, Leicester, York, Exeter)
Defence Animal Centre (Melton Mobray)
RAVC Support Group (Aldershot)
Resettlement Centres (Catterick & York)
College of Military Education & Training Services (Beaconsfield)
Cadet Training Centre

Smaller Corps

THE INTELLIGENCE CORPS (Int Corps) - The Int Corps deals with operational intelligence, counter intelligence and security.

THE ROYAL ARMY VETERINARY CORPS (RAVC) - The RAVC look after the many animals that the Army has on strength. Veterinary tasks are mainly directed towards guard or search dogs and horses for ceremonial duties.

THE ARMY PHYSICAL TRAINING CORPS (APTC) - Consists mainly of SNCOs who are responsible for unit fitness. The majority of major units have a representative from this corps on their strength.

THE GENERAL SERVICE CORPS (GSC) - A holding unit for specialists. Personnel from this corps are generally members of the reserve army.

SMALL ARMS SCHOOL CORPS (SASC) - A small corps with the responsibility of training instructors in all aspects of weapon handling.

CHAPTER 11 - UNITS OF THE ARMY

The Cavalry

Accounts for about 6% of the strength of the Army and, after the re-organisation following the Options for Change review, will be organised into 11 armoured regiments and one mounted ceremonial regiment as follows:

The Household Cavalry

The Household Cavalry Regiment	HCR
The Household Cavalry Mounted Regiment	HCMR

The Royal Armoured Corps

1st The Queen's Dragoon Guards	QDG
The Royal Scots Dragoon Guards	SCOTS DG
The Royal Dragoon Guards	RDG
The Queen's Royal Hussars	QRH
9th/12th Royal Lancers	9/12L
The King's Royal Hussars	KRH
The Light Dragoons	LD
The Queen's Royal Lancers	QRL
1st Royal Tank Regiment	RTR
2nd Royal Tank Regiment	RTR

Permanent Locations:

United Kingdom -	5 Regiments (including HCMR)
Germany -	7 Regiments

The Infantry

About 25% of the Army which, after reorganisation following the Options for Change review, will be divided into 41 general service battalions, plus six battalions of The Royal Irish Regiment which will be used only in Northern Ireland and The Special Air Service Regiment.

The Guards Division

1st Bn The Grenadier Guards	1 GREN GDS
1st Bn The Coldstream Guards	1 COLM GDS
1st Bn The Scots Guards	1 SG
1st Bn The Irish Guards	1 IG
1st Bn The Welsh Guards	1 WG

There are generally three battalions from the Guards Division on public duties in London at any one time. In March 1995 these three battalions were 1st Bn The Grenadier Guards, 1st Bn The Scots Guards and 1st Bn The Irish Guards. 1st Bn The Coldstream Guards are deployed as an armoured infantry battalion with 1 (UK Division) in Germany and 1st Bn The Welsh Guards are a general service battalion stationed at Tern Hill in Shropshire. When a Regiment is stationed in London on public duties it is given an extra company to ensure the additional manpower required for ceremonial events is available.

The 2nd Bns of the Grenadier, Coldstream and Scots Guards have been placed in suspended animation.

The Scottish Division

1st Bn The Royal Scots	1 RS
1st Bn The Royal Highland Fusiliers	1 RHF
1st Bn The King's Own Scottish Borderers	1 KOSB
1st Bn The Black Watch	1 BW
1st Bn The Argyll & Sutherland Highlanders	1 A and SH
1st Bn The Highlanders	1 HLDRS

The Queen's Division

1st Bn The Princess of Wales's Royal Regiment (Queen's and Royal Hampshire)	1 PWRR
2nd Bn The Princess of Wales's Royal Regiment (Queen's and Royal Hampshire)	2 PWRR
1st Bn The Royal Regiment of Fusiliers	1 RRF
2nd Bn The Royal Regiment of Fusiliers	2 RRF
1st Bn The Royal Anglian Regiment	1 R ANGLIAN
2nd Bn The Royal Anglian Regiment	2 R ANGLIAN

The King's Division

1st Bn The King's Own Royal Border Regiment	1 KINGS OWN BORDER
1st Bn The King's Regiment	1 KINGS
1st Bn The Prince of Wales's Own Regiment of Yorkshire	1 PWO
1st Bn The Green Howards	1 GREEN HOWARDS
1st Bn The Queen's Lancashire Regiment	1 QLR
1st Bn The Duke of Wellington's Regiment	1 DWR

The Prince of Wales Division

1st Bn The Devonshire & Dorset Regiment	1 D and D
1st Bn The Cheshire Regiment	1 CHESHIRE
1st Bn The Royal Welch Fusiliers	1 RWF
1st Bn The Royal Regiment of Wales	1 RRW
1st Bn The Royal Gloucestershire, Wiltshire and Berkshire Regiment	1 RGWBR
1st Bn The Worcestershire & Sherwood Foresters Regiment	1 WFR
1st Bn The Staffordshire Regiment	1 STAFFORDS

The Light Division

1st Bn The Light Infantry	1 LI
2nd Bn The Light Infantry	2 LI
1st Bn The Royal Green Jackets	1 RGJ
2nd Bn The Royal Green Jackets	2 RGJ

The Brigade of Gurkhas

1st Bn The Royal Gurkha Regiment	1 RGR
2nd Bn The Royal Gurkha Regiment	2 RGR
3rd Bn The Royal Gurkha Regiment	3 RGR

In 1996/97 2 RGR and 3 RGR will amalgamate to form 2 RGR leaving only two Gurkha battalions in the Army - 1 RGR and 2 RGR. Following (1995) closure of the Training Depot, Brigade of Gurkhas in Hong Kong, recruits will be trained at Church Crookham in Hampshire under the wing of the resident UK Gurkha Battalion.

The Parachute Regiment

1st Bn The Parachute Regiment	1 PARA
2nd Bn The Parachute Regiment	2 PARA
3rd Bn The Parachute Regiment	3 PARA

The Royal Irish Regiment

1st Bn The Royal Irish Regiment	1 R IRISH
3rd/4th/5th/7th/8th/9th Royal Irish Regiment*	3-9 R IRISH

* The 3rd to 8th Bns The Royal Irish Regiment are employed exclusively in Northern Ireland and were formerly battalions of The Ulster Defence Regiment . The 4/5 Rangers is a TA Battalion stationed in Northern Ireland and wearing the Royal Irish capbadge.

134

Infantry Battalions - Permanent Locations

United Kingdom	-	31 Battalions
Germany	-	6 Battalions
Cyprus	-	2 Battalions
Hong Kong	-	1 Battalion
Brunei	-	1 Battalion

The Special Air Service Regiment

The 22nd Special Air Service Regiment   22 SAS

The SAS can be classed as an infantry unit but the members of the regiment are found from all arms and services in the Army after exhaustive selection tests.

The Support Arms

The Royal Regiment of Artillery   RA
About 10% of the Army.

1st Regiment Royal Horse Artillery	1 RHA	(Field)
3rd Regiment Royal Horse Artillery	3 RHA	(Field)
4th Regiment	4 REGT	(Field)
5th Regiment	5 REGT	(MLRS)
7th Regiment Royal Horse Artillery	7 RHA	(Parachute)
12th Regiment	12 REGT	(Air Defence)
14th Regiment	14 REGT	(Training)
16th Regiment	16 REGT	(Air Defence)
17th Regiment	17 REGT	(Training)
19th Regiment	19 REGT	(Field)
22nd Regiment	22 REGT	(Air Defence)
26th Regiment	26 REGT	(Field)
29th Commando Regiment	29 REGT	(Field)
32nd Regiment	32 REGT	(MLRS)
39th Regiment	39 REGT	(MLRS)
40th Field Regiment	40 REGT	(Field)
47th Regiment	47 REGT	(Air Defence)

Permanant Locations - at late 1995
United Kingdom - 11 Regiments
Germany - 5 Regiments

MLRS Regiments are stationed at Catterick and Larkhill. The third MLRS Regiment currently stationed in Germany will return to the UK in late 1995 when it will be stationed at Ouston near Newcastle-Upon-Tyne.

The Corps of Royal Engineers   RE
About 8% of the Army.

1st RSME Regiment	1 RSME REGT RE
3rd RSME Regiment	3 RSME REGT RE
21st Engineer Regiment	21 ENGR REGT
22nd Engineer Regiment	22 ENGR REGT
25th Engineer Regiment	25 ENGR REGT
28th Engineer Regiment	28 ENGR REGT
32nd Engineer Regiment	32 ARMD ENGR REGT
33rd Engineer Regiment	33 ENGR REGT (EOD)
35th Engineer Regiment	35 ENGR REGT
36th Engineer Regiment	36 ENGR REGT
38th Engineer Regiment	38 ENGR REGT
39th Engineer Regiment	39 ENGR REGT
The Queens Gurkha Engineers	QGE

Permanent Locations

United Kingdom	-	8 Regiments
Germany	-	4 Regiments
Hong Kong	-	1 Regiment

The total for the UK includes the 2 x RSME Training Regiments.

The Royal Corps of Signals   R SIGNALS
About 9% of the Army.

1st (UK) Armd Div HQ and Signal Regiment	1 SIG REGT
2nd Signal Regiment	2 SIG REGT
3rd (UK) Div HQ & Signal Regiment	3 SIG REGT
7th (ARRC) Signal Regiment	7 SIG REGT
9th Signal Regiment	9 SIG REGT
11th Signal Regiment (Trg Regt)	11 SIG REGT
14th Signal Regiment (Electronic Warfare)	14 SIG REGT
15th Signal Regiment	15 SIG REGT
16th Signal Regiment	16 SIG REGT
30th Signal Regiment	30 SIG REGT
Queens Gurkha Signals	QG SIGNALS

Permanent Locations

United Kingdom	-	6 Regiments
Germany	-	3 Regiments
Cyprus	-	1 Regiment
Hong Kong	-	1 Regiment

During late 1995 the total in Germany will fall to 3 Regiments whem 14 Signal Regiment returns to the UK. The Regiment will be located at the former RAF station at Brawdy in Wales.

The Army Air Corps   AAC

1st Regiment	1 REGT AAC
3rd Regiment	3 REGT AAC
4th Regiment	4 REGT AAC
7th Regiment	7 REGT AAC
9th Regiment	9 REGT AAC

Permanent Locations

United Kingdom	-	4 Regiments
Germany	-	1 Regiment

THE SERVICES

The Royal Logistic Corps (RLC)
Approximately 16% of the Army.

1 General Support Regiment	1 (GS) REGT
2 Close Support Regiment	2 (CS) REGT
3 Close Support Regiment	3 (CS) REGT
4 General Support Regiment	4 (GS) REGT
5 Territorial Army Training Regiment	5 (TRG) REGT (V)
6 Support Regiment	6 (SP) REGT
7 Transport Regiment	7 (TPT) REGT
8 Artillery Support Regiment	8 (ARTY SP) REGT
9 Supply Regiment	9 (SUP) REGT
10 Transport Regiment	10 (TPT) REGT
11 Explosive Ordnance Disposal Regiment	11 (EOD) REGT
12 Supply Regiment	12 (SUP) REGT
14 Supply Regiment	14 (SUP) REGT
17 Port and Maritime Regiment	17 (PORT) REGT
21 Logistic Support Regiment	21 (LOG SP) REGT
23 Pioneer Regiment	23 (PNR) REGT
24 Regiment	24 REGT

27 Transport Regiment	27 (TPT) REGT
29 Regiment	29 REGT
Queen's Own Gurkha Transport Regiment*	GTR

There is a Commando Logistic Regiment with the Royal Marine's 3 Commando Brigade that has a number of RLC personnel included amongst its personnel and 5 Airborne Brigade has its own Close Support battalion with large numbers of RLC personnel. By mid 1995 the RLC Regimental presence in Germany was 7 Regiments:

1 General Support Regiment	-	Gutersloh
2 Close Support Regiment	-	Gutersloh
6 Support Regiment	-	Gutersloh
7 Transport Regiment	-	Bielefeld
12 Supply Regiment	-	Wulfen
14 Supply Regiment	-	Dulmen
24 Regiment	-	Bielefeld

* It is expected the the Queen's Gurkha Transport Regiment will be reduced to squadron strength before 1997.

Royal Army Medical Corps (RAMC)

Has the following Regular Army field medical units:

1 Armoured Field Ambulance	1 ARMD FD AMB
2 Armoured Field Ambulance	2 ARMD FD AMB
3 Armoured Field Ambulance	3 ARMD FD AMB
16 Armoured Field Ambulance	16 ARMD FD AMB
24 Armoured Field Ambulance	24 ARMD FD AMB
4 Field Ambulance	4 FD AMB
5 Field Ambulance	5 FD AMB
19 Airmobile Field Ambulance	19 AIRMOB FD AMB
23 Parachute Field Ambulance	23 PARA FD AMB
21 Field Hospital	21 FD HOSP
33 Field Hospital	33 FD HOSP
34 Field Hospital	34 FD HOSP
84 Field Medical Equipment Depot	84 FMED

Other Corps

Royal Army Medical Corps (RAMC) - Provides 13 x Regular field ambulance or hospitals.
Corps of Royal Electrical & Mechanical Engineers (REME) - Provides 5 x Equipment Support Bns and large numbers of detachments. The majority of major units have REME sub-units under command.

The Adjutant General's Corps - Generally detachments to formed units.
The Royal Army Chaplains' Department (RAChD) - Individual detachments.
Royal Army Veterinary Corps (RAVC) - Detachments.
Small Arms School Corps (SASC) - Detachments & School Staff.
Royal Army Educational Corps (RAEC) - Detachments & Army Garrison
Education Centres.
Royal Army Dental Corps (RADC) - Detachments.
Intelligence Corps (Int Corps) - Detachments at various command levels.
Army Physical Training Corps (APTC) - Detachments & School Staff.
General Service Corps (GSC) - Reserve Pool.
Army Legal Corps (ALC) - Generally individual detachments.
Queen Alexandra's Royal Army Nursing Corps (QARAC) - Generally providing
staff a medical centres and hospitals.

The Territorial Army (TA) - Situation 1 March 1995

At the beginning of 1995 the TA was approximately 68,500 strong. TA soldiers are
part-time volunteers, and many are very experienced, first class soldiers
who will be expected to take their place alongside the regular formations in any
future conflict. Although some members of the TA are organised in specialised,
sponsored units the majority are members of larger independent units among which
are:-

Cavalry

The Royal Yeomanry	RY
The Queen's Own Yeomanry	QOY
The Royal Wessex Yeomanry	R WX Y
The Royal Mercian & Lancastrian Yeomanry	R ML Y
The Scottish Yeomanry	SCOT Y

Artillery

Honourable Artillery Company	102 AD Regt
100 Fd Regt	103 AD Regt
101 Fd Regt	104 AD Regt

Infantry

Scottish Division	Queens Division	
1/52 Lowland	5 PWRR	5 R Anglian
2/52 Lowland	6/7 PWRR	6 R Anglian
1/51 Highland	Londons	7 R Anglian
2/51 Highland	5 RRF	
3/51 Highland	6 RRF	

Kings Division

4 King's Own Border
5/8 King's
4 QLR
3 PWO
3 DWR
4/5 Green Howards

Light Division

5 LI (V)
6 LI (V)
7 LI (V)
8 LI (V)
4 RGJ
5 RGJ

21 SAS & 23 SAS

Prince of Wales's Division

1 Wessex	3 WFR
2 Wessex	3 Staffords
4 D & D	3 Cheshire
3 RWF	
3/4 RRW	

Parachute Regiment

4 Para
10 Para

The Royal Irish Regiment

4/5 Rangers

Engineers

R MON RE	75 Engr Regt
71 Engr Regt	76 Engr Regt
72 Engr Regt	77 Engr Regt
73 Engr Regt	101 Engr Regt (EOD)
74 Engr Regt	111 Engr Regt

Signals

31 (Special Tasks) Sig Regt
32 (Scottish) Sig Regt
33 (Lancashire & Cheshire) Sig Regt
34 (Northern) Sig Regt
35 (South Midland) Sig Regt
36 (Eastern) Sig Regt 37 (Wessex and Welsh) Sig Regt
38 Signal Regiment
71 (Yeomanry) Signal Regiment

Logistics

15 (Western) Supply Regiment RLC
16 (Eastern) Supply Regiment RLC
18 (Scottish) Supply Regiment RLC
19 (Southern) Supply Regiment RLC

86 Postal and Courier Regiment RLC
87 Postal and Courier Regiment RLC
88 (Scottish) Postal and Courier Regiment RLC
89 Postal and Courier Regiment RLC
150 (Yorkshire) Transport Regiment RLC
151 (Greater London) Transport Regiment RLC
152 (Ulster) Ambulance Regiment RLC
Scottish Transport Regiment RLC
156 (North West) Transport Regiment RLC
157 (Wales and Midland) Transport Regiment RLC
161 Ambulance Regiment RLC
162 Movement Control Regiment RLC

The Gibraltar Regiment

Consists of one infantry company and an artillery battery which assists in the
defence of Gibraltar. We believe that there are plans to convert this regiment into
an all infantry organisation for the defence of Gibraltar following the withdrawal of
the last regular resident infantry battalion in 1991.

TA Reorganisation

At the end of 1994 the UK MoD announced a wide ranging re-organisation of the
TA that if anything appears to have enhanced its role and almost certainly ensures
its long term survival. In general terms the TA will be formed in larger numbers of
smaller units, and personnel will be part of either high readiness or ready reserve
formations. The majority of the changes to the TA will be in place by 1 April 1996
and the broad outline of these changes is as follows:

Royal Armoured Corps

1 x Armoured Reconniassance Regiment
1 x NBC Defence Regiment
4 x National Defence Reconniassance Regiments
1 x Independent National Defence Reconnaissance Squadron
1 x Armoured Delivery Regiment

The Royal Yeomanry will re-role to form the NBC Defence Regiment equipped
with Fuchs and Saxon armoured vehicles. The 8th Bn The Light Infantry will
re-role as a National Defence Reconnaissance Regiment and the Queens Own
Yeomanry will convert to the new Sabre CVR(T) vehicle. The armoured delivery
regiment will form at the RAC Centre, Bovington to provide crews for replacement
armoured vehicles and to deliver them to the front line.

Royal Artillery
2 x Field Regiments (FH-70)

3 x Air Defence Regiments (Javelin)
1 x Airmobile Battery (Light Gun)
1 x Commando Battery (Light Gun)
1 x Airborne Battery (Light Gun)
Honourable Artillery Company

Royal Engineers
5 x General Support Regiments
3 x Air Support Regiments
1 x Explosive Ordnance Disposal Regiment
1 x Commando Squadron
1 x Topographic Squadron
1 x Independent Field Park Squadron
1 x Field Park Squadron
Civil Affairs Organisation
Military Works Force

The Civil Affairs Organisation will be formed to co-ordinate host nation and other military support for running the infrastructure of a large civilian community and will consist of specialists in a wide field of skills.

Royal Signals
3 x Ptarmigan Regiments
2 x Euromux Regiments
6 x National Communications Regiments
3 x Independent Signals Squadrons
2 x Special Communications Squadrons

The 2 (National Communications)Brigade units will be restructured to provide Regional and National Communications support to Land Command. An independent Combat Service Support Group Squadron will also be formed.

Infantry
In the future all TA Infantry Battalions, including Parachute Battalions, will have a common establishment of three Rifle Companies and a Headquarters Company. In addition there will be 4 x Fire Support Battalions with mortar, Milan and machine gun platoons. Following re-organisation there will be:

29 x General Reserve TA Battalions
4 x Fire Support Battalions

To effect these changes the 1st and the 2nd Battalions of the Wessex Regiment will merge. The 8th Battalion of the Light Infantry will form a National Defence Reconnaissance Regiment and elements of the Royal Anglian Regiment will for the new Independent Transport Regiment leaving 2 x Royal Anglian Battalions in the Order of Battle. There are more details in Chapter 5.

Army Air Corps
1 x Aviation Regiment

Royal Logistic Corps
1 x HQ Transport Group
1 x HQ Postal and Courier Group
8 x Transport Regiments
2 x Ambulance Regiments
3 x Postal and Courier Regiments
1 x Supply Regiment
1 x Pioneer Regiment
1 x Port Regiment
2 x Movement Control Regiments
1 x Catering Support Regiment
1 x Training Regiment
19 x Specialist Squadrons

These changes will result in the formation of 3 x Transport Regiments, 1 x Port
Regiment, 1 x Movement Control Regiment, 1 x Rear Support Company and 1 x
Combat Service Support Battalion Squadron.

Army Medical Services
11 x Field Hospitals
7 x Field Ambulances
1 x Parachute Medical Squadron
1 x Ambulance Train Group
13 x Specialist Medical Teams
1 x Field Medical Equipment Depot

Field Hospitals will now be restructured to consist of a Headquarters with 2 x
Surgical Teams with 100 beds and 2 x sub-units each with 1 x Surgical Team and 50
beds.

Royal Electrical & Mechanical Engineers
5 x Equipment Support Battalions

Military Bands
Following re-organisation of military bands by 1 April 1995 the Regular Army will
have 30 bands employing some 1,143 bandsmen.

Household Cavalry	-	70 musicians	-	2 bands
Grenadier Guards	-	49 musicians	-	1 band
Coldstream Guards	-	49 musicians	-	1 band
Scots Guards	-	49 musicians	-	1 band
Welsh Guards	-	49 musicians	-	1 band

Irish Guards	-	49 musicians	-	1 band
Royal Artillery	-	49 musicians	-	1 band
Royal Engineers	-	35 musicians	-	1 band
Royal Signals	-	35 musicians	-	1 band
Royal Logistic Corps	-	35 musicians	-	1 band
REME	-	35 musicians	-	1 band
Adjutant General's Corps	-	35 musicians	-	1 band
Army Air Corps	-	35 musicians	-	1 band
Royal Armoured Corps	-	140 musicians	-	4 bands
Scottish Division	-	70 musicians	-	2 bands
Queens Division	-	70 musicians	-	2 bands
Kings Division	-	70 musicians	-	2 bands
Prince of Wales's Division	-	70 musicians	-	2 bands
Light Division	-	49 musicians	-	1 band
Parachute Regiment	-	35 musicians	-	1 band
Royal Irish Regiment	-	35 musicians	-	1 band
Royal Gurkha Rifles	-	35 musicians	-	1 band

There are 24 bands in the Territorial Army.

CHAPTER 12 - Recruiting, Selection and Training

Captain Plume: The army is the place to make men of you: every man has his lot, and you have yours. What think you now of a purse full of French gold out of a monsieur's pocket, after you have cracked him over the head with your firelock, eh?

Costar Pearmain: I'll have it Captain - give me a shilling and I'll follow you to the end of the world.

The Recruiting Sergeant - George Farquhar 1678-1707

Recruiting can best be described as the steps taken to attract sufficient men and women of the right quality to meet the Army's personnel requirements. Selection is the process that is carried out to ensure that those who are accepted into the Army have the potential to be good soldiers and are capable of being trained to carry out their chosen trade. Training is the process of preparing those men and women for their careers in the Army. Training is progressive and continues all the way through a soldier's career.

Recruiting

The Director General Army Manning and Recruiting (DGAMR), a Major General in The Ministry of Defence, is responsible for ensuring that the Army is properly manned and that sufficient men and women of the right quality are recruited to meet the needs of the service.

An MOD committee called the Standing Committee Army Manpower Forecasts (SCAMF) calculates the numbers that need to be enlisted to maintain the Army's personnel at the correct level. The Committee needs to take account of changing unit establishments, wastage caused by servicemen and women leaving the service at the end of their engagements, and those who might choose to leave before their engagements come to an end (PVR - Premature Voluntary Retirement). The number required in each trade in the Army is assessed and figures are published at six monthly intervals so that adjustments may be made during the year.

The Director of Army Recruiting (DAR), a Brigadier in The Ministry of Defence, and his staff located throughout the United Kingdom are then responsible for the recruiting and selection to meet the personnel targets.

Potential recruits are attracted into the Army in a number of ways including advertisements on the television, in cinemas and in the press. Permanently established recruiting teams from many Regiments and Corps tour the country and staff from the Army Careers Information Offices (ACIOs) visit schools, youth clubs and job centres. Young, recently trained soldiers are also sent back to their home towns and schools to talk to their friends about life in the Army and are regularly interviewed by the local press.

Figures for the Army alone are not available, but during 1993-94 the total cost of recruiting for all three services was £96.71 million when 11,949 recruits entered the services from civilian life. Of this total 9,576 entered the Army and the average cost of recruiting each trainee was £8,093. During late 1994 there were 251 service careers information offices in the UK.

Annual Army recruiting figures during the recent past are as follows:

	1990/91	1991/92	1992/93	1993/94
Officers	1,454	1,364	1,064	752
Soldiers	16,048	15,774	10,323	8,824

During the year 1995-1996 we believe that the Army plans to recruit some 1,200 officers and over 15,700 soldiers.

Soldier Selection

Potential recruits are normally aged between 16 years and 6 months and 25 years, except when they are applying for a vacancy as an apprentice when the age limits are from 15 years 8 months to 17 years 6 months.

Under the latest selection system a potential recruit will have a preliminary assessment at the ACIO. Here he or she will take the computer based Army Entrance Test (AET) which is designed to assess ability to assimilate the training required for the candidate's chosen trade. The staff at the ACIO will conduct a number of interviews to decide on overall suitability for the Army. The ACIO staff will look at references from school or any employers and offer advice on which trade may be available and might suit the candidate. A preliminary medical examination will also be carried out that checks on weight, eyesight and hearing. If the test and interviews are successfuly passed the candidate will be booked for further tests at the Recruit Selection Centre which is closest to his or her home. Recruit selection centres are at Glencorse in Scotland, Litchfield in Staffordshire, Pirbright in Surrey and Ballymena in Northern Ireland.

The candidates will remain at the RSC for an overnight stay and undergo another medical examination, a physical assessment test and an interview with a Personnel Selection Officer. The potential recruit will also see at first hand the type of training that they will undergo and the sort of life that they will lead in barracks if successful in getting into the Army. Physical fitness is assessed based on a timed run and some gymnasium exercises. After further interviews the candidate is informed if he or she is successful and if so is offered a vacancy in a particular trade and Regiment or Corps.

Phase 1 Training

Basic Recruit or Phase 1 training is the same for all soldiers whatever Regiment or Corps and whichever trade they are enlisted into. The course lasts for 10 weeks and is called The Common Military Syllabus (Recruit) (CMSR). It includes training in the basic military skills required of all soldiers and incorporates Weapon Handling and Shooting, Drill, Physical Fitness, Field Tactics, Map Reading, Survival in Nuclear Chemical and Biological Warfare and General Military Knowledge. It is an intensive course and requires the recruit to show considerable determination and courage to succeed.

The Army training organisation carries out centralised Phase 1 Training at 5 Army Training Regiments (ATRs). Each ATR is responsible for training all recruits enlisting into the following Regiments and Corps (with the exception of apprentices).

ATR Pirbright - The Household Cavalry, Infantry of the Guards Division, The Royal Logistic Corps, the Royal Electrical and Mechanical Engineers and the Royal Artillery.

ATR Bassingbourne - The Royal Engineers, The Royal Signals and Infantry of the Queen's Division.

ATR Winchester - The Royal Armoured Corps, Infantry of the Light Division, The Army Air Corps, The Adjutant General's Corps (including the Royal Military Police) and The Intelligence Corps.

ATR Glencorse - Infantry of the Scottish and King's Divisions.

ATR Lichfield - Infantry of the Prince of Wales's Division, The Parachute Regiment, Royal Army Medical Corps, Royal Army Veterinary Corps, Royal Army Dental Corps and Queen Alexandra's Royal Army Nursing Corps.

Phase 1 Training for the Royal Irish Regiment takes place at Ballymena in Northern Ireland.

Gurkha recruits now trained at Church Crookham following the closure of the Training Depot Brigade of Gurkhas in Hong Kong. The first intake of 153 men selected from 57,000 applicants will start training in the UK during early 1995.

Phase 2 Training

Phase 2 training is the 'Special to Arm' training that is required to prepare soldiers who have recently completed their basic Phase 1 training, to enable them to take their place in field force units of their Regiment or Corps. This phase of training has no fixed period and courses vary considerably in length. As an example infantry

Phase 2 training is reported to take 11 weeks.

Phase 2 training for the major Arms and Services is carried out as follows:

The Royal Armoured Corps - Takes place at Bovington Camp in Dorset. Recruits into the Household Cavalry Regiment also undergo equitation training.

Infantry - From May 1995 all infantry recruits will do their Phase 2 Training at the Infantry Training Battalion in Catterick.

The Royal Artillery - At the Royal School of Artillery at Larkhill in Wiltshire.

The Royal Engineers - Cove in Hampshire and at the Royal School of Military Engineering at Chatham in Kent.

The Royal Logistic Corps - Drivers are trained at Leconfield, supply specialists at Blackdown, Cooks at Aldershot and Pioneers at Northampton.

The Adjutant General's Corps - Pay and Clerks are trained at the AGC Depot at Worthy Down near Winchester and the Royal Military Police at Chichester.

Royal Electrical and Mechanical Engineers - Vehicle Mechanics are trained at Bordon and other trades at Arborfield.

Royal Signals - Training takes place at the Royal School of Signals at Blandford in Dorset.

Royal Army Medical Corps - At the RAMC Depot at Keogh Barracks, Aldershot.

Apprentices Phase 1 and Phase 2 training which can last for up to two years is conducted at the Army Apprentice College. On entry Apprentices are generally aged between 16 years and 17 years and 6 months.

Commissions

There are two main types of commission in the Army. These are:

a. THE REGULAR COMMISSION (Reg C) which is for those who wish to make the Army their permanent career. Regular Officers can normally expect their career to last until their 55th birthday.
b. THE SHORT SERVICE COMMISSION (SSC) which is for those who remain uncertain about their long-term career plans. The SSC lasts for a minimum of 3 years (6 for the Army Air Corps) but can be extended if mutually agreed to a maximum of 8 years.

The minimum educational requirements for a Regular Officer are currently 5 passes at GCSE which must include English Language, Mathematics and either a Science subject or Modern Language. Two of the passes must be at 'A' level grades A to E. Some Corps only accept candidates with appropriate degrees or professional qualifications.

The requirements for a Short Service Commission are less stringent requiring only 5 passes at GCSE grades A-C including English Language or Mathematics. Candidates for commissions should be over 17 years and 9 months and under 25 years old when they begin officer training.

c. SHORT SERVICE LIMITED COMMISSION - The SSLC is a commission that is aimed at those who have completed their 'A' Levels and have a gap year prior to entering University. The selection procedure at RCB has to be completed after which a three week course at Sandhurst is attended. Those who successfully complete the course join their chosen Regiment or Corps as 2nd Lieutenants for a minimum of 4 months and a maximum of 18 months with a front-line unit, but not on active service. The purpose of the SSLC is to create a pool of young men and women who will take a favourable impression of the Army into their careers.

d. LATE ENTRY COMMISSIONS - A number of vacancies exist for senior Non Commissioned Officers and Warrant Officers to be granted commissions known as Late Entry Commissions. Officers commissioned from the ranks are initially employed in exactly the same way as those granted direct entry commissions but because of their age, generally do not rise above the rank of Major.

Officer Selection & Sandhurst

Candidates for commissions are normally advised by a Schools or University Liaison Officer of the options open to them and who arranges for interviews and familiarisation visits to an appropriate Regiment or Corps. If the Regiment or Corps is prepared to sponsor a candidate they then guide him or her through the rest of the selection procedure. All candidates are required to attend the Regular Commissions Board (RCB) at Westbury, Wiltshire for a three day assessment prior to which they should have undergone a medical examination and attended a pre-RCB briefing so that they know what to expect.

RCB consists of a series of interviews and tests that assess the personality and the leadership potential in applicants. There is no secret in the selection procedures and details are available for all applicants.

RCB may, in some cases require further development in either leadership skills or academic standards prior to beginning officer training, and this is conducted on a 12 week course at Rowallan Company at The Royal Military Academy Sandhurst (RMAS) which is at Camberley in Surrey.

All potential officers accepted for training attend the RMAS Common

Commissioning Course at Sandhurst which lasts for 44 weeks with 3 entries a year in January, May and September. Both graduates and non-graduates attend the same commissioning course. After successfully completing the Sandhurst course a young officer then completes a further specialist course with his or her chosen Regiment or Corps. Later in their careers, in addition to technical, special to arm courses, officers attend the Junior Division of the Staff College course at Warminster and if selected the Army Staff Course at Camberley.

Females cannot be accepted in the Household Cavalry, The Royal Armoured Corps or the Infantry. Also some other Regiments and Corps restrict the number of vacancies open to women.

Welbeck College

Welbeck is the Army's sixth form college which offers two year 'A' Level courses for boys and girls who wish to gain commissions in the technical Corps. The Welbeck course is science and engineering based and as it includes leadership training, Welbexians do not need to attend the Regular Commissions Board but simply require the recommendation of the Headmaster to gain entry to RMAS.

Army Training Overview

Responsible for Army Training is the Inspectorate General of Doctrine and Training (IGDT) based at Upavon in Wiltshire employing about 18,000 service and civilian personnel (the majority in the UK and Germany) with a budget of over £500 million annually. HQ IGDT has 103 military staff and 116 civilian personnel and is directly responsible to the Adjutant General.

Following basic Phase 1 and Phase 2 training soldiers are posted to their units and progressive training is carried out on a continual basis. Training is geared to individual, sub-unit or formation level and units regularly train outside of the UK and Germany. As would be expected there are specialist unit training packages for specific operational commitments such as Northern Ireland and Yugoslavia.

For example the training package for personnel warned off for deployment to the former Yugoslavia consists of a 12 day special-to-mission package. The training is carried out by specialist training advisory teams at the Army's Combined Arms Training Centre at Warminster and for Germany based units at the Sennelager Training Centre.
The British Army's main training areas outside of the Europe are:

Canada - Suffield

British Army Training Unit Suffield (BATUS) has the responsibility to train battlegroups in the planning and execution of armoured operations through the medium of live firing and tactical test exercise. There are 6 x "Medicine Man" battlegroup exercises each year in a training season that lasts from March to November.

Canada - Wainright

The British Army Training Support Unit at Wainright (BATSU(W)) provides the logistic and administrative support for Infantry units at the Canadian Forces training base in Western Canada. During the winter months the unit moves in its entirety to Fort Lewis in the USA where it carries out a similar function. There are usually 3 battalion group exercises at Wainright and 2 at Fort Lewis during the course of each training year.

Kenya

British Army Liaison Staff Kenya (BATLSK) is responsible for supporting Infantry battalion group exercises and approximately 3,000 British troops train in Kenya each year in a harsh unforgiving terrain ranging in altitude from 8,000 feet down to 2,300 feet. BATLSK has been based at its present site in Kahawa Barracks since Kenya's independence in 1963.

Belize

The British Army Training Support unit Belize (BATSUB) was formed on 1 October 1994. Its role is to give training and logistic support to Land Command units training in a tropical jungle environment. During its first full year of operation BATSUB will cost £3.1 million.

During 1993/1994 training exercises were also carried out in Australia, Botswana, Brunei (4 x company level exercises), Jamaica, Jordan, Cyprus (22 x company level exercises), Hawaii, Malaysia, and New Zealand.

Overseas Students

During the 1993-1994 financial year, 4,566 students from 98 different countries took part in training in the United Kingdom. The charges for training depend on the length of the course, its syllabus and number taking part. Receipts from overseas governments for this training were believed to be in the region of £39,500,000, during 1993-94.

Training Standards

Shooting - All ranks are required to take an annual personnel weapons test (APWT). Pass rates for 1992/93 were:

Infantry	-	98%
Royal Armoured Corps	-	85%
Royal Engineers	-	74%
Royal Artillery	-	78%

Royal Signals	-	88%
Royal Logistic Corps	-	89%
Army Average	-	86%

Basic Fitness Test - All soldiers of all ranks and ages are required to take a basic fitness test. This test involves a 1.5 mile run and walk (in a squad) on level ground and in training shoes, in 10 minutes for those under 30. There are gradually rising time limits for older personnel and recruits in training are given 10 mins and 30 seconds for the 1.5 mile run. The current standards for women are lower and female recruits are allowed to do the 1.5 mile run in 12 minutes and 50 seconds.

Recruit Training Assessments - During Recruit Training personnel are assessed at different stages of training as follows:

Test	Introduction	Interim	Final
Heaves	2	4	6
Sit Up Test	1 Min (20 reps)	2 min (42 reps)	3 min (65 reps)
1.5 Mile Run	11 min 30 sec	11 mins	10 min 30 sec

Career Profile - Soldier

As an illustration of the career that might be expected for a regular soldier, we have used a model based on the career of Thomas Atkins. A serving soldier about to retire after 22 years' service.

Age

17 - Left school at 16. Bored with life at home and not happy in his job with British Rail. Decides to join the Army, and takes selection tests at his local Army Careers Office. After a successful assessment at the Recruit Selection Centre he is sent to an Army Training Regiment to complete Phase 1 Common Military Syllabus (Recruit) Training lasting ten weeks. Following completion of the course he attends the Infantry Training Centre at Catterick for a further 12 week course where the specialist infantry skills are taught. After initial training Atkins is posted to a regular battalion of his regiment which is serving in Cyprus. Spends 18 months in Cyprus where he is employed as a rifleman in an infantry platoon.

19 - The battalion is posted to Tidworth in Hampshire. Rfn Atkins is transferred from an infantry platoon in "A" Company to the Anti-Tank Platoon in Support Company. Atkins sees this move as a career advancement, and from Tidworth completes a 6-month tour in Belize and a 6-month tour in Ulster. About two and a half years after arriving in Tidworth the battalion is posted to Belfast on an 18-month tour.

21 - Directly after the move to Belfast Rfn Atkins attends a battalion NCOs training course and is promoted to Lcpl. As a Lcpl he is the 2ic of an infantry

section in a rifle platoon operating in some of the most dangerous parts of the city. After a year in Belfast, he is promoted to Cpl and attends a Weapons Instructors Course lasting 8 weeks at the School of Infantry in Wiltshire.

23 - The battalion leaves Belfast on posting to Germany as an armoured infantry battalion mounted in Warrior armoured fighting vehicles. Cpl Atkins is posted to the Army Training Regiment where he is responsible for training a section of recruits. After two years at the Army Training Regiment he re-joins his battalion that has two years of its four year tour left to serve.

25 - Spends one year in Germany commanding an infantry section mounted in a Warrior AIFV during which time the battalion spends six months on operations in support of the UN in Bosnia. At the end of this year attends a Platoon Sergeants Course at the School of Infantry, and on rejoining the battalion after the course is promoted Sergeant.

26 - Becomes 2ic of a rifle platoon, is responsible for the "on the job" training of a young officer and the welfare of the 35 soldiers in his care. On occasions, he commands the platoon in the absence of the officer platoon commander.

30 - Promoted to Colour Sergeant and becomes an instructor at the Royal Military Academy Sandhurst where he teaches officer cadets some of the fundamentals of soldiering. After Sandhurst, returns to the battalion now serving in Cyprus where he runs the logistical support for an infantry company.

33 - Promoted WOII (Company Sergeant Major) and is almost entirely responsible for the discipline and administration of an infantry company of about 130 men.

36 - Appointed RQMS (Regimental Quartermaster Sergeant) and is now responsible for much of the logistic support for a complete infantry battalion.

38 - Promoted WOI (Regimental Sergeant Major). The most senior soldier in the battalion and very much the Commanding Officer's right hand man. Much feared by the scruffy and the idle, avoided by young officers with long hair, the reputation of the battalion is his personal responsibility.

40 - At the end of his service leaves the Army and returns to civilian life.

Note: Not all RSM's return to civilian life at the end of 22 years service. Many are offered commissions and fill important posts in both regiments and corps, often as Quartermasters responsible for equipment worth many millions of pounds. For example the Quartermaster of a cavalry regiment may be responsible for tanks, armoured vehicles and associated items on charge to the regiment worth some £250 million. As long ago as the First World War, Field Marshal Sir William Robertson (a commissioned warrant officer) became Chief of the Imperial General Staff.

Career Profile - Officer

To illustrate an officer's career, we have used a non graduate regular officer who has elected to serve in the infantry.

Age

19 - Having left school with 2 A Levels decides to join the Army and goes to the Regular Commissions Board (RCB) at Westbury in Wiltshire to undergo selection. On being passed by the RCB as a suitable candidate for a commission, is given a date to start at the Royal Military Academy, Sandhurst (RMA). At the RMA he completes a one year course, designed to give young officers a sound basic military education. Following graduation from Sandhurst he attends the 12 week Platoon Commanders Battle Course at the School of Infantry.

20 - Posted to a battalion of his Regiment as a 2/Lt. The battalion is serving in Catterick and he commands a rifle platoon for two years. During his tour as a platoon commander the battalion serves in South Armagh on a six month tour and takes part in an exercise in Kenya. After two years is promoted to Lt.

22 - Posted to the Infantry Training Centre where he commands a number of Training Platoons during a two year posting. Training Platoons usually have experienced regular NCOs as instructors and their task is to take soldiers from the Army Training Regiments and turn them into infantrymen during a 12 week course.

24 - Returns to the battalion and commands the Mortar Platoon for a further 18 months, having undergone a conversion course at the School of Infantry. At the end of this period is selected to become the Battalion Adjutant and is responsible for the day-to-day discipline and administration of the battalion.

27 - On appointment as Adjutant he is promoted Captain.

29 - After two years as Adjutant he is posted away from the battalion, and spends the next two years as an infantry exchange officer in the United States.

31 - Returns to the battalion now serving in Germany and becomes the 2i/c of an armoured infantry company. During this time he starts to prepare himself for an examination which if he passes will qualify him for promotion to Major, and if he does extremely well will qualify for a place at the staff College.

32 - Becomes the Battalion Operations Officer, responsible to the Commanding Officer for preparing the battalion's war plans. Passes the Staff/Promotion exam and is given a place at the Staff College.

33 - Attends a course at the Staff College Camberley. After one year at the Staff College is promoted to major and posted to HQ 5th Division as a staff officer in the Operations Branch (SO2 G3)

36 - Returns to the battalion now serving in Tidworth where he commands a mechanised rifle company (mounted in Saxon APCs) for two years. During this period the battalion serves on six month tour in support of the UN in Bosnia.

38 - Posted to HQ 1(UK) Armoured Division where he fills a staff officer's post in the Training Branch.

39 - Selected for promotion to Lt Col and returns to the battalion once again serving in Germany. He now commands a Battlegroup composed of tanks, infantry, artillery and engineers.

42 - Promoted to Colonel and becomes a staff officer at JHQ Northwood working for the Director of Military Operations.

47 - Is promoted to Brigadier and commands a Armoured Brigade in Germany.

50 - Commands a Division in the Allied Rapid Reaction Corps (ARRC) as a Major General.

55 - Retires as a Lieutenant General to become a television personality. Is constantly seen on BBC Newsnight commenting on newsworthy crisis situations.

CHAPTER 13 - Some Aspects of the Future Battlefield

"We continue to believe that through 2020-2040 future US Army & Marine Corps operations will be earth based".

> US National Defence University Briefer.

"The moment they all start shouting it can't be done I know it's already happening".
Arthur C Clarke.

General

All the old "certainties" regarding the size and shape of the battlefield that modern armies may have to contend with have evaporated. The increasing use of helicopters, and a perceived decrease in the utility of armour suggest a fundamental change in the employment of all battlefield systems during the next 25 years.

The forward edge of the battlefield of the future is likely to be a fluid and rapidly changing arena, where conventional front lines and areas of friendly or enemy territory are difficult to identify, and where highly intelligent sensors are employed to enable commanders at all levels to monitor and control the situation that the ebb and flow of the battle dictates. In the past, C3I (Command, Control, Communications and Intelligence) has been a slow and laborious business. In the not too distant future, the high technology employed in battlefield C3I systems will probably make the current in-service technology resemble that of 1914.

Within the next 20 years we expect the area of the future battlefield to be much larger than that of today. This area over which the single related military action that we know as a battle can be fought, will only be constrained by communications, and this large battlefield will probably have a sparse military population, with access to large amounts of real time intelligence and some extremely sophisticated weapons. In addition to the current airborne and satellite surveillance systems, information will be fed into command modules via emplaced and remotely delivered sensors, and highly mobile (generally heliborne) forces will react to events and attempt to seize ground or destroy the enemy.

The usefulness of anti-armour weapons will almost certainly decrease in line with the reductions in the numbers of armoured vehicles employed - especially main battle tanks. However, in the final analysis we see no alternative to infantry capturing and holding ground and this infantry, although far fewer numerically than hitherto, will probably remain part of an all arms grouping, remaining equipped with a high technology rifle and its accessories as their personal battle fighting system. However, the barriers between soldier, weapon and communications package are collapsing.

Throughout the Western world there is a considerable amount of activity aimed at establishing what has been described as "The Intelligent Battlefield". The aim of this activity is to merge current and future technology with battlefield requirements, providing a high tech solution to problems such as increased battlefield mobility, the massive increase in battlefield information and perceived falls in manpower levels.

Technology

Recent technological advances that are almost certain to have a major impact on the future battlefield are amongst the following:

Miniaturisation & Communications

We would expect the current trends in miniaturisation to continue, with electronic equipment in the C3I sector continuing to get smaller, lighter, and becoming capable of processing larger amounts of data even more rapidly than currently possible. We are probably looking forward to a period where almost instant secure communications are available throughout the battlefield, and down to the level of the smallest sub-unit. The 'fog of war' and the lack of information available to a commander is already being replaced by the problem of "fog of too much information" and how to filter out what is really relevant.

Communications down to the smallest sub-unit level are already a fact. Secure, hand held communication devices weighing no more than a couple of pounds are already available, and we will see their widespread introduction into service during the next decade. These devices will probably be ECM resistant and their overall effect will probably be to increase the size of the area over which a unit can effectively operate. In addition, remote sensors, including real time TV linked to the C3I chain will enhance surveillance over this increased battlefield area.

Sensor technology is moving forward fast, and there is a wide variety of extremely small sensors available, capable of being delivered to all areas of the battlefield by either helicopters, aircraft or RDMs. The latest generation of RDMs (remotely delivered munitions) has given the commander on the ground the ability to react to changes in both the nature and direction of the threat at the very last moment, especially when delivered at long ranges from a system such as the MLRS.

Remote sensors the size of a tennis ball will be able to monitor adjacent areas, identify movement (and type) in their area, send digital information to their control station and if necessary detonate munitions in the vicinity of a nearby (certainly within 2 or 3 kms) target. A future battlefield could be sown with thousands of these sensors, each of them interacting in a massive, secure, communications network.

Digitisation

Digitisation refers to putting the capabilities for digital communications into a platform. Digital modulation is the process of encoding a continuous analog signal into a discontinuous signal. Then numerical codes consisting of discrete on (one) and off (zero) pulses are assigned to represent a measure of the basic signal. The measuring process involves sampling the amplitude of the continuous signal at intervals and transmitting a digital code to represent the amplitude. The same process can be used in data transmissions where digital codes represent letters and numbers. Linking platforms from aircraft to mines and sensors on the ground in an intelligent circuit allows these systems to interact automatically on a continual flow of information around the circuit.

Linked to digitisation, the next trend in communications is probably towards secure image transmission linking information from humans and sensors. For example, a platoon commander's sketch map of the current situation in his area can be transmitted simultaneously to the company, battalion, brigade and divisional headquarters and either modified or confirmed by sensor information. This map could then be scanned into the overall C3I system and both humans and sensors made aware of the results. Time spent in talking about the situation on the air and the possibility of confusion and misunderstandings are dramatically reduced.

Surveillance

Both miniaturisation and communications have impacted on surveillance systems as previously mentioned. The 24 hour, high intensity battlefield is already a fact and amongst the first division military nations, there is already a real ability to operate effectively by night and by day.

In the immediate future surveillance will continue to be real time and with a 24 hour capability. In the longer term surveillance systems will be linked to remotely controlled (and probably remotely delivered) munitions such as mines, and could be controlled from command posts at a great distance from the scene of the action. For example, intelligent mines laid to protect a vulnerable point in the Gulf could be monitored, and if necessary detonated from a headquarters in the UK. Intelligent mines could themselves become a valuable link in the surveillance chain, notifying their headquarters of the approach of potential targets and the state of their particular area of the battle.

Ability to React

Another of the main technology drivers on the shape of the future battlefield is the ability to react rapidly to information received. Aviation technology has produced the attack helicopter, and early types such as the US Cobra and Russian Mi-24 Hind, have already been replaced by the AH-64 Apache and

Mi-28 Havoc. The attack helicopter has challenged the main battle tank as the most dominant equipment on the current battlefield, and we expect this trend to continue.

Currently the UK Army Air Corps has about 350 helicopters in its inventory, and is the only organisation that appears to have been increased in size following the United Kingdom's 'Options for Change' proposals. By the end of the decade this organisation could be further increased as other organisations (such as heavy armoured units) are reduced. In the medium term we would expect to see the UK establishing more than just 1 x airmobile brigade (currently 24 Air Mob Bde) and we would expect to see the Royal Marines 3 Cdo Brigade, becoming totally airmobile.

The US Army is already airmobile with a tactical doctrine to suit. Other armies are following on and a battlefield mobility revolution has been underway for the past decade. The helicopter allows for the mobility required to react to incidents at a distance, without large numbers of troops spread over a wide area. Remote surveillance devices allow for monitoring of areas at great distance. The two are complimentary and change the commander's area of influence at all levels of command, from the platoon to the division.

The advent of the attack helicopter equipped with anti-tank guided missiles means that in the future the number of main battle tanks on the battlefield will be reduced. This is already happening in all of the first division military nations, and over the next decade we would see the figure of main battle tanks in the inventory continuing to decrease. However, we believe that small numbers of main battle tanks, and larger numbers of light armoured fighting vehicles will remain in service to exploit situations where armed/attack helicopter operations might be either unsuitable or impossible. In addition light armoured vehicles may adopt a role of a "mobile electronics rebroadcast/intelligence filter" designed to update local units on low power or local loop transmissions.

Possible Scenario

In the not too distant future it is possible to envisage an operational area sewn with sensors that identify an enemy airmobile attack hundreds of kilometres away. The sensors identify the enemy helicopter force and call for the delivery of "intelligent" anti-helicopter mines/munitions/systems capable of differentiating between friendly or enemy helicopters, and long range artillery delivers these mines onto likely enemy approach routes. At the same time the "immediate" reaction force becomes heliborne and acting on sensor information moves to engage the now depleted enemy on their landing zone. Infantry will still be required to finally destroy the enemy on the ground.

The Infantry

In the light of modern technological developments we believe that the infantry will be one of the few major military growth areas during the next twenty five years. Generally speaking, the basic infantry in the majority of the world's defence forces resembles the infantry of 1914. They are trained to walk long distances, tactics are broadly similar and they fire personal weapons with ranges that are almost identical to those of 1914.

In many countries, the infantry are carried into battle by either armoured personnel carriers or helicopters, but the basic equipment and type of soldier employed in the role remain very much as it was 75 years ago. Even the training period (on average 8-12 weeks for most nations) remains much the same.

Karl von Clausewitz's "Army of Mass" and the modern conscript army is threatened by a number of factors:

The first of these is the social background of recruits. In the past the infantry was the great majority in any army and the mass of recruits came from agricultural communities. Today, and especially in the industrial countries, the mass of recruits come from an urban background. The US Infantry has already identified a high percentage of this urban youth as "untrainable couch potatoes," many of whom are so unfit that they are incapable of walking more than a couple of kilometres without assistance. In addition the tough mental attitude required in sound infantry has been "educated" out of many of these individuals. The situation is the same in Europe. Men who can be properly trained as athletes, stalkers and marksmen are becoming harder to find.

The second is economics. The British estimate the running costs of a basic private soldier as being in the region of £7,000 per year (excluding salary). Figures like these are bearable for small regular armies but the same ones apply for large conscript armies in industrialised countries, and the cost is becoming a burden that is proving difficult to bear. There is a problem here for defence planners, money is short and they must choose between people or equipment. Generally speaking they will choose equipment before people, with the rationale for this choice being - if you have the equipment it will be in place in a time of emergency. People can always be trained within a few weeks, but the war fighting equipment will take much longer to produce. The difficulty is actually finding the time to train the people in an emergency.

The third is public opinion and at this moment the military are very much out of fashion. Modern society finds it extremely difficult to cope with the sight of young conscripts far from home dying on their television screens, especially on a UN Operation such as Somalia. Currently the only really acceptable way of operating is by the use of professional regular infantry, and as their use becomes more widespread, the number of tasks that this infantry are required to do multiplies.

The result of this is much higher standards of infantry training, further reducing the size of the manpower pool from which this infantry can be recruited.

The twenty four hour, 2 dimensional battlefield, where units can move 50kms in as many minutes calls for an extra skill to the infantryman's repertoire. Wavell's description of the ideal infantry soldier as being a cat burglar, poacher and gunman needs the addition of the skills of a technologically literate "computer hacker". In the not too distant future the infantry soldier is going to have access through a personal battle station - probably consisting of digitally interactive miniaturised electronics in the butt of his rifle, and if he is unable to handle the technology, the effort and expense will be useless.

However, no-matter what social, political, military and economic changes impact upon the battlefield, at the bottom line the infantry soldier's final defence is his personal weapon - the rifle.

Some Thoughts on the Future Rifle

The rifle as a weapon that fires bullets into the atmosphere via a barrel and towards a target, has probably "gone about as far as it can go," arriving at the end of its current developmental path.

Future developments will be in dazer/lasers, "intelligent" sighting systems and integrated sensors, detectors and communications systems. These developments will be designed to assist the infantry soldier in acquiring and hitting his target, with the rifle itself becoming an important active/interactive sensor on the future battlefield.

Non-lethal weapons (other than lasers) probably do not have a place on the battlefield. However, they almost certainly have important applications in law enforcement and internal security operations and will probably follow their own developmental line.

The future battlefield might be an area that could initially be subjected to a "silent bombardment" of remotely delivered sensors. These sensors will feed the battlefield's digital communications loop, and the infantry soldier's weapon will probably interact with these semi-intelligent systems to acquire and destroy targets.

Short Term Developments

We believe that in the immediate future the development of the rifle will be influenced by the following factors:

a. The introduction into service of a battlefield dazer - there will almost certainly be calls for a hand held dazer/laser to be produced in Europe, probably mounted in tandem with a current 5.56mm rifle. A reasonably effective weapon could be manufactured in the UK - possibly within a five year period. Trials are already taking place of such a weapon in the US.

b. Work will almost certainly begin on semi-intelligent sighting systems designed to assist in target acquisition. The initial efforts will probably be centred around a designator, with some form of mini-computer designed to account for the battlefield variables.

c. European manufacturers and Defence Ministries will be closely monitoring US attempts to establish a digital information loop into battlefield communications systems. It is very possible that some form of IFF system and NBC warning device will be incorporated into small arms before the end of the century, and such systems could be "netted" into a prototype communications loop within a very short time.

d. Work on battlefield sensors will continue in both Europe and the US with the bulk of the work being done in the US. Within five years a rudimentary form of "enemy in close proximity" device will probably appear - with a high probability that it will be a component of the rifle. In the initial stages such a device would probably be an outstation of an interactive armoured vehicle, parked in close proximity.

e. Post 2000AD the developments that we have already outlined will be improved upon and there will be a move towards total integration of the rifle with the "intelligent battlefield" concept. This integration will probably be a steady evolutionary move, with a rifle in service between 2025 and 2050 that resembles the model in the final part of this section.

A Glimpse of the Future Rifle

The rifle of 2044 will be instantly recognisable to the soldier of the 1990s. The SA-EU40 (manufacturer Euroarms) will almost certainly weigh under 5kg and be less than 1 metre in length. In addition we believe that it has a high percentage chance of remaining capable of discharging a conventional bullet - probably of 5.56mm calibre or smaller. However, the emerging battlefield technology will have made its impact.

This evolutionary weapon will be the individual infantry soldier's battle-station. Built around the bullet discharging mechanism, will be a host of miniaturised systems designed to maximise the potential of the individual infantry soldier and act as a force multiplier for his capabilities. The infantry soldier has the potential to become the "Super Trooper".

Built into the area of the butt will be a communications device, linked into the sensors of the intelligent battlefield system via the digital loop. This digital communications device will allow the individual soldier to communicate with all levels of command, and will also enable commanders to either page or constantly be aware of the location of each soldier via the battlefield digital loop.

A small high powered dazer/laser will probably be mounted on the top of the weapon. This dazer/laser will be effective for M kills on enemy soldiers at ranges of 400 to 1000 metres, and designed primarily to damage vulnerable organs such as eyes but having a secondary function in degrading high technology equipment. K kills at shorter ranges will be achieved using conventional bullets fired down the barrel.

The really astonishing changes will be in the sighting system and its associated technological package. The system will be interactive with the battlefield digital loop and probably incorporate:

a. Telescopic sight with 24 hour - all weather vision, variable zoom and a real time TV processing image to the command and control units via the digital loop.

b. A central computer that is voice activated.

c. The infantry soldier will be able to access all battlefield systems through the digital communications loop. For example a map of the tactical situation in front of his position will be available, and real time TV of the next "tactical bound," obtained from ground sensors, helicopters and satellites etc will be available through his sight.

d. The rifle is interactive with emplaced battlefield sensors. These sensors will warn his sighting system when an enemy has been detected and indicate the position of the enemy inside his arc of responsibility via a "flashing arrow" on the sight screen. When and if the enemy appears, a predictor will automatically "aim off" for movement, and the sight will automatically adjust for wind and elevation via a target designator. In addition, the infantry soldier will conceivably carry a number of miniature sensors, that he could either place in front of a static position or fire out to about 1,000 metres via a rifle grenade type attachment.

e. Interactive communications will ensure that Command and Control units are automatically informed that Fire Team Alpha, of 6 Platoon, 1 BLANKSHIRE BG is in contact, has fired 300 rounds and taken 1 casualty. In the rear depots replacement ammunition will start its "just in time" journey to the forward units, and the medevac proceedure from battlefield casualty collection to a field hospital bed will be activated. The replacement soldier for the casualty, will be briefed on the tactical situation via his rifle information system as he moves forward to take his place in the line.

f. Via the sight realtime images of the situation will be capable of transmission throughout the command and control chain. The soldier will be able to show his commander what he can see through his sight.

The rifle will almost certainly incorporate a GPS indicator and carrying a map will probably become an activity of the past. Maps will be accessible via the sighting system.

An integral mine detector designed to give warning of surface laid scatterable anti-personnel mines could be incorporated. An IFF device and an NBC warning monitor could also be incorporated probably operating on bio-sensors. In the longer term, by making the rifle so important to the soldier's survival, it becomes more unlikely that personnel under pressure would be willing to part with their weapons.

To enhance his ability as a battlefield hunter, the rifleman of the future is going to be an extremely capable operator of high technology equipment, and the rifle will almost certainly be the most important item amongst this equipment. In all probability the majority of future "Super Trooper's" high technology accessories will eventually be operated through the rifle, with the weapon acting as the core of the system.

Afterthoughts

We appreciate that we have been "crystal ball gazing" but the developmental work for many of these enhancements is being carried out now, and some of the more outlandish ideas are not as far away as many would believe. The British Army being what it is - we know two things that will certainly happen. The infantry believing (quite rightly in our opinion) in the effectiveness of "cold steel" will demand that any future rifle is fitted with a bayonet boss, and the Brigade of Guards will spend many long hours rewriting the pamphlet for Drill and Ceremonial.

CHAPTER 14 - MISCELLANEOUS

The Military Hierarchy

Rank	Badge	Appointment Example
General (Gen)	Crown, Star & Crossed Sword with Baton	Adjutant General
Lieutenant General (Lt Gen)	Crown & Sword & Baton	Commander ARRC
Major General (Maj Gen)	Star & Sword & Baton	Divisional Commander
Brigadier (Brig)	Crown & 3 Stars	Brigade Commander
Colonel (Col)	Crown & 2 Stars	Staff or School Commandant
Lieutenant Colonel (Lt Col)	Crown & 1 Star	Battle Group/Armoured Regiment/Infantry Bn Commander
Major (Maj) Captain (Capt)	Crown 3 Stars	Sqn/Coy/Bty Commander Squadron/Company 2ic
Lieutenant (Lt)	2 Stars	Troop/Pl Commander
2nd Lieutenant (2/Lt)	1 Star	Troop/Pl Commander
Warrant Officer First Class	Royal Coat of Arms on Forearm	Regimental Sergeant Major (WO 1) (RSM)
Warrant Officer Second Class	Crown on Forearm	Company Sergeant Major (WO 2) (CSM)
Staff Sergeant (Ssgt)	Crown over 3 stripes	Coy/Sqn Stores (or Colour Sergeant)
Sergeant (Sgt)	3 stripes	Platoon Sergeant
Corporal (Cpl)	2 stripes	Section Commander
Lance Corporal	1 Stripe	Section 2ic (Lcpl)

Modes of Address
Where appropriate soldiers are addressed by their generic rank without any

qualifications, therefore Generals, Lieutenant Generals and Major Generals are all addressed as "General". Colonels and Lieutenant Colonels as "Colonel", Corporals and Lance Corporals as "Corporal". Staff Sergeants and Colour Sergeants are usually addressed as "Staff" or "Colour" and CSMs as Sergeant Major. It would almost certainly be prudent to address the RSM as "Sir".

Private Soldiers should always be addressed by their title and then their surname. For example: Rifleman Harris, Private Jones, Bugler Bygrave, Gunner Smith, Guardsman Johnson, Sapper Williams, Trooper White, Kingsman Doyle, Signalman Robinson, Ranger Murphy, Fusilier Ramsbotham , Driver Higgins, Craftsman Sewell or Air Trooper Steptoe. However, it should be remembered that regiments and corps have different customs and although the above is a reasonable guide it may not always be correct.

Regimental Head-Dress

The normal everyday head-dress of NCOs and Soldiers (and in some regiments of all ranks) is the beret or national equivalent. The norm is the dark blue beret. Exceptions are as follows:

a.	Grey Beret	The Royal Scots Dragoon Guards Queen Alexandra's Royal Army Nursing Corps
b.	Brown Beret	The King's Royal Hussars The Royal Wessex Yeomanry
c.	Khaki Beret	All Regiments of Foot Guards The Honourable Artillery Company The Kings Own Royal Border Regiment The Royal Anglian Regiment The Prince of Wales's Own Regiment of Yorkshire The Green Howards The Duke of Wellington's Regiment
d.	Black Beret	The Royal Tank Regiment
e.	Rifle Green Beret	The Light Infantry The Royal Green Jackets The Brigade of Gurkhas Adjutant General's Corps.
f.	Maroon Beret	The Parachute Regiment
g.	Beige Beret	The Special Air Service Regiment

h.	Light Blue Beret	The Army Air Corps	
i.	Scarlet Beret	Royal Military Police	
j.	Cypress Green Beret	The Intelligence Corps	

The majority of Scottish Regiments wear the Tam-O-Shanter (TOS) and the Royal Irish Regiment wear the Corbeen.

Regular Army Rates of Pay as at lst April 1995

Officers	On Appointment	Rising To
University Cadet	7,635	10,741
Second Lieutenant	13,315	-
Lieutenant	17,600	19,454
Captain	22,509	26,166
Major	28,564	34,229
Lieutenant Colonel	40,270	44,504
Colonel	46,891	51,826
Brigadier	57,578	

Notes:

(1) Rates of pay apply to both male and female officers.
(2) QARANC Officers are commissioned as Lieutenants.

Adult Soldiers	Band	Scale A (£ per week)	£ per Annum
Private Class 4	1	159.88	8,336
Private Class 3	1	179.13	9,340
Private Class 3	2	207.97	10,844
Private Class 3	3	239.96	12,512
Private Class 2	1	200.27	10,442
Private Class 2	2	228.69	11,957
Private Class 2	3	261.38	13,629
Private Class 1	1	217.84	11,358
Private Class 1	2	246.82	12,869
Private Class 1	3	278.81	14,537
Lance Corporal Class 1	1	250.32	13,052
Lance Corporal Class 1	2	279.37	14,567
Lance Corporal Class 1	3	314.02	16,373
Corporal Class 1	1	288.54	15,045

Rank				
Corporal Class 1	2	**317.52**	**16,556**
Corporal Class 1	3	**352.24**	**18,366**
Sergeant	5	350.28	18,264
Staff Sergeant	5	368.48	19,213
Warrant Officer Class 2	6	434.63	22,662
Warrant Officer Class I	7	501.69	26,159

Notes:

(1) Pay scales apply to both males and females. (2) These rates only show the most common basic pay rates. (3) From the 1st January 1991 all recruits have been enlisted on an Open Engagement. The Open Engagement is for a period of 22 years service from the age of 18 or the date of enlistment whichever is the later. Subject to giving 12 months notice, and any time bar that may be in force, all soldiers have the right to leave on the completion of 3 years reckonable service from the age of 18.

Length of Service Increments (LSI)

Daily Rates - After 9 years service personnel are eligible for extra daily long service increments of pay. These vary according to rank.

Rank	9 yrs	12 yrs	15 yrs	18 yrs	22 yrs
	£	£	£	£	£
Pte	0.79	1.12	1.12	1.12	1.12
LCpl	0.79	1.12	1.12	1.12	1.12
Cpl	0.79	1.12	1.36	1.36	1.36
Sgt	0.96	1.36	1.68	1.99	1.99
SSgt	0.96	1.36	1.68	2.31	2.31
WO2	0.96	1.36	1.68	2.31	2.64
WO1	0.96	1.36	1.68	2.31	3.03

Soldiers Pay Bands

All employments in the Army are grouped into Bands for calculating pay. Band 1 includes all recruits during training and the majority of employments. In general, the more skilled the employment, the higher the pay band.

Examples of Band 2 Employments are - Bandsman; Farrier; Driver Tank Transporter; Radar Operator(RA); Command Post Asistant(RA); Meteorologist; OP Assistant (RA); Surveyor(RA); Armoured Engineer; Amphibious Engineer; Bomb Disposal Engineer; Telecom Op (Linguist); Telecom Op (Systems); Student Nurse; Op Theatre Technician; Pharmacy Technician; Dental Technician; Operator Special Intelligence; Armourer; Blacksmith; Bricklayer; Carpenter; Construction Materials Technician; Draughtsman; Driver Specialist (RE); Electrician; Fitter; Gun Fitter; Metalsmith; Painter; Plant Operator; Plumber;

Printer; Railwayman; Sheetmetal Worker; Shipwright; Vehicle Electrician; Vehicle Mechanic; Welder; Well Driller.

Examples of Band 3 employments are - Survey Technician; Telecom Op (Telegraph); Laboratory Technician; Physiological Measurement Technician; Registered General Nurse; Registered Mental Nurse; Telecom Op (Special); Telecom Technician; Physiotherapist; Aircraft Technician; Control Equipment Technician; Radar Technician; Marine Engineer; Radiographer; Avionics Technician; Instrument Technician; SAS Soldier.

Junior Entrants

Age	£ per week	£ per annum
16 but under 16.5 yrs	99.61	5,193
16.5 but under 17 yrs	99.61	5,193
17 but under 17.5 yrs	120.89	6,303
17.5 years and over	159.88	8,336

Food charges	£ per Day
Standard food charge	2.99
Married Unaccompanied Food Charge	2.20

Single Accommodation Charges (Grade 1)	£ per Day
Major and Above	3.88
Captain & Below	3.24
Senior NCO	2.36
Cpl and Below	1.37
Junior Soldiers	1.07

Additional Pay	£ per Day
Parachutists All ranks	3.44
Parachute Jump Instructors All ranks	4.94

Aircrewmen	£ per Day
Initial rate	4.50
Middle rate	9.93
Top rate	11.67

Officer Pilots & Flying Instructors - Flying Pay -	£ per Day

Initial Rate	9.09
Middle rate	15.26
Top rate	23.06
Lt Col after 6 years	21.82
Lt Col after 8 years	20.53
Colonel on appointment	19.24
Colonel after 2 years	17.95
Colonel after 4 years	16.68
Colonel after 6 years	14.77
Colonel after 8 years	12.83
Brigadier	7.69

Soldiers Pilots and Flying Instructors - Flying Pay -	£ per Day
Initial rate	9.09
Middle rate	15.26
Top rate	23.06

South Georgia Pay	£ per Day
All ranks	4.13

Northern Ireland Pay	£ per Day
All ranks	4.13

Experimental Pay	£ per Day
All ranks per test	1.73

Separation Allowance	£ per Day
UK and NW Europe	3.75
Elsewhere	2.92

The Royal Marines

Although the Royal Marines (RM) are an organisation that is part of the Royal Navy, they are trained and equipped for warfare on land, and it is very likely that they could be involved in operations and exercises with Army units. The Royal Marines number approximately 7,500 officers and men and their primary task is the reinforcement of Norway and NATO's Northern Flank, should a threat develop in that area.

The Royal Marines also have detachments on 12 ships at sea and a number of smaller units world-wide with widely differing tasks. However, the bulk of the manpower of the Royal Marines is grouped in battalion sized organisations known as Commandos (Cdo). There are 3 Commando Groups and they are part of a larger formation known as 3 Commando Brigade

3 Cdo Bde.

HQ 3 Cdo Bde
(Plymouth)

40 Cdo	42 Cdo	45 Cdo	29 Cdo Regt RA
(Taunton)	(Plymouth)	(Arbroath)	(Plymouth) (1)

Cdo Logistics Regt	Cdo Bde Air Sqn	59 Cdo Sqn RE
(Plymouth)	(Yeovilton)	(Plymouth)

Note: (1) 29 Cdo Regt RA has one battery stationed at Arbroath with 45 Cdo.

Commando Organisation
Cdo HQ

Rifle Coy	Rifle Coy	Rifle Coy	Support Coy	HQ Coy
				Signals
				Transport
				Medical

Survey	Recce	Mortar Tp	Anti-Tank Tp	Engr
Tp	Tp	6x81mm Mor	12 Milan	Tp

Note: A troop (Tp) equates to an army platoon. Each rifle company has three troops.

RAF Regiment

Currently the RAF Regiment exists to provide ground and short range air defence for RAF installations, and to train all of the RAF's combatant personnel to enable them to contribute to the defence of their units. During late 1993, the strength of the RAF Regiment was approximately 3,000 (including 264 officers). Following restructuring, strength is believed to be planned to be at about 2,400 by late 1995.

As of 1 Jan 1995 RAF Regiment units are as follows:

No 1 Group

| No 2 Squadron | - | RAF Honnington | - | Field Squadron |
| No 3 Squadron | - | RAF Aldergrove | - | Field Squadron |

No 2 Group

No 1 Squadron	-	RAF Laarbruch	-	Field Squadron
No 26 Squadron	-	RAF Laarbruch	-	Rapier
No 37 Squadron	-	RAF Bruggen	-	Rapier

No 11 Group

No 15 Squadron	-	RAF Leeming	-	Rapier
No 27 Squadron	-	RAF Leuchars	-	Rapier
No 48 Squadron	-	RAF Lossiemouth	-	Rapier

No 6 Wing (For deployment in support of USAF)

No 19 Squadron	-	RAF Brize Norton	-	Rapier
No 20 Squadron	-	RAF Honnington	-	Rapier
No 66 Squadron	-	RAF Honnington	-	Rapier

Independent Units

No 63 (QCS)	-	RAF Uxbridge	-	Ceremonial/Field Squadron
No 34 Squadron	-	RAF Akrotiri	-	Field Squadron
RAF Regiment Depot	-	RAF Honnington		
Rapier Training Unit	-	RAF Honnington		

There are now two basic RAF Regiment squadron organisations - the field squadron organised for ground defence against possible enemy ground action and the rapier squadron organised for defence against low-flying enemy aircraft. There are four dedicated field squadrons and 63 (QCS) Squadron with a dual ceremonial/field squadron role. Five rapier squadrons defend RAF airbases and three rapier squadrons have a role in defending USAF bases in the UK.

Rapier Squadron-Possible Organisation

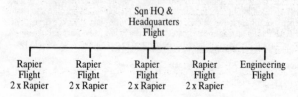

172

Codewords and Nicknames

A Codeword is a single word used to provide security cover for reference to a particular classified matter, eg "Corporate" was the Codeword for the recovery of the Falklands in 1982. In 1990 "Granby" was used to refer to operations in the Gulf and Op Grapple is used for current operations in support of the UN in the former Yugoslavia. A Nickname consists of two words and may be used for reference to an unclassified matter, eg "Lean Look" referred to an investigation into various military organisations in order to identify savings in manpower.

Dates and Timings

When referring to timings the British Army uses the 24 hour clock. This means that 2015 hours, pronounced twenty fifteen hours, is in fact 8.15pm. Soldiers usually avoid midnight and refer to 2359 or 0001 hours. Time zones present plenty of scope for confusion! Exercise and Operational times are expressed in Greenwich Mean Time (GMT) which may differ from the local time. The suffix Z (Zulu) denotes GMT and A (Alpha) GMT + 1 hour. B (Bravo) means GMT + 2 hours and so on.

The Date Time Group or DTG can be seen on military documents and is a point of further confusion for many. Using the military DTG 1030 GMT on 20th April 1995 is written as 201030Z APR 95. When the Army relates days and hours to operations a simple system is used:

a. D Day is the day an operation begins.
b. H Hour is the hour a specific operation begins.
c. Days and hours can be represented by numbers plus or minus of D Day

Therefore if D Day is the 20th April 1995, D-2 is the 18th April and D + 2 is the 22nd April. If H Hour is 0600hrs then H+2 is 0800 hours.

Phonetic Alphabet

To ensure minimum confusion during radio or telephone conversations difficult words or names are spelt out letter by letter using the following NATO standard phonetic alphabet.

ALPHA - BRAVO - CHARLIE - DELTA - ECHO - FOXTROT - GOLF - HOTEL - INDIA - JULIET - KILO - LIMA - MIKE - NOVEMBER - OSCAR - PAPA - QUEBEC - ROMEO - SIERRA - TANGO - UNIFORM - VICTOR - WHISKEY - X RAY - YANKEE - ZULU.

Military Quotations - Useful For Use on Briefings etc

"You will usually find that the enemy has three courses open to him, and of these he will adopt the fourth."

Anon.

"No plan survives contact with the enemy."

Herman Von Molkte 1800-91

"The military value of a partisan's work is not measured by the amount of property destroyed, or the number of men killed or captured, but the number he keeps watching."

John Singleton Mosby 1833-1916
Confederate Cavalry Leader

"Peace - In international affairs, a period of cheating between two periods of fighting."

The Devils Dictionary 1911

"The number of medals on an officers breast varies in inverse proportion to the square of the distance of his duty from the front line."

Charles Montague 1867-1928

"The analysts write about war as if its a ballet. Yes, it's choreographed, and what happens is, the orchestra starts playing and some son of a bitch climbs out of the orchestra pit with a bayonet and starts chasing you around the stage. And the choreography goes right out of the window".

General Norman Schwarzkopf.

"If wars were won by feasting,
Or victory by song,
Or safety found in sleeping sound,
How Britain would be strong".

Rudyard Kipling

"Have I not myself known five hundred living soldiers, sabred into crow's meat for a piece of cotton which they call their colour; which had you sold it in any market cross would not have bought above three pence".

Thomas Carlyle 1834

"Hell hath no fury like a non-combatant".

Charles Montague 1867-1928

Abbreviations

The following is a selection from the list of standard military abbreviations and should assist users of this handbook.

AWOL	Absent without leave
accn	Accommodation
ACE	Allied Command Europe

Adjt	Adjutant
admin	Administration
admin O	Administrative Order
ac	Aircraft
AD	Air Defence/Air Dispatch/Army Department
ADA	Air Defended Area
ADP	Automatic Data Processing
AFCENT	Allied Forces Central European Theatre
AIFV	Armoured Infantry Fighting Vehicle
Airmob	Airmobile
ATAF	Allied Tactical Air Force
armr	Armour
armd	Armoured
ACV	Armoured Command Vehicle
AFV	Armoured Fighting Vehicle
AMF(L)	Allied Mobile Force (Land Element)
APC	Armoured Personnel Carrier
APDS	Armour Piercing Discarding Sabot
ARV	Armoured Recovery Vehicle
AVLB	Armoured Vehicle Launched Bridge
AP	Armour Piercing/Ammunition Point/Air Publication
APO	Army Post Office
ARRC	Allied Rapid Reaction Corps
ATGW	Anti Tank Guided Weapon
ATWM	Army Transition to War Measure
arty	Artillery
att	Attached
BE	Belgium (Belgian)
BGHQ	Battlegroup Headquarters
bn	Battalion
bty	Battery
BK	Battery Captain
BC	Battery Commander
BG	Battle Group
bde	Brigade
BAOR	British Army of the Rhine
BFG	British Forces Germany
BFPO	British Forces Post Office
BMH	British Military Hospital
C3I	Command, Control, Communications & Intelligence.
cam	Camouflaged
cas	Casualty
CCP	Casualty Collecting Post
CCS	Casualty Clearing Station
CASEVAC	Casualty Evacuation
cat	Catering

CAD	Central Ammunition Depot
CEP	Circular Error Probable/Central Engineer Park
CEPS	Central European Pipeline System
CET	Combat Engineer Tractor
CVD	Central Vehicle Depot
CW	Chemical Warfare
COS	Chief of Staff
civ	Civilian
CP	Close Protection/Command Post
CAP	Combat Air Patrol
c sups	Combat Supplies
CV	Combat Vehicles
CVR(T) or (W)	Combat Vehicle Reconnaissance Tracked or Wheeled
comd	Command/Commander
CinC	Commander in Chief
CPO	Command Pay Office/Chief Petty Officer
CO	Commanding Officer
coy	Company
CQMS	Company Quartermaster Sergeant
comp rat	Composite Ration (Compo)
COMSEN	Communications Centre
coord	Co-ordinate
CCM	Counter Counter Measure
DAA	Divisional Administrative Area
DTG	Date Time Group
def	Defence
DF	Defensive Fire
DK	Denmark
dml	Demolition
det	Detached
DISTAFF	Directing Staff (DS)
div	Division
DAA	Divisional Administrative Area
DMA	Divisional Maintenance Area
DS	Direct Support/Dressing Station
ech	Echelon
EME	Electrical and Mechanical Engineers
ECCM	Electronic Counter Measure
emb	Embarkation
EDP	Emergency Defence Plan
EMP	Electro Magnetic Pulse
en	Enemy
engr	Engineer
EOD	Explosive Ordnance Disposal
eqpt	Equipment
ETA	Estimated Time of Arrival

EW	Early Warning/Electronic Warfare
ex	Exercise
FRG	Federal Republic of Germany
FGA	Fighter Ground Attack
fmm	Formation
FUP	Forming Up Point
FAC	Forward Air Controller
FEBA	Forward Edge of the Battle Area
FLET	Forward Location Enemy Troops
FLOT	Forward Location Own Troops
FOO	Forward Observation Officer
FR	France (French)
FRT	Forward Repair Team
FUP	Forming Up Place
GDP	General Defence Plan
GE	German (Germany)
GR	Greece (Greek)
GOC	General Officer Commanding
GPMG	General Purpose Machine Gun
hel	Helicopter
HE	High Explosive
HEAT	High Explosive Anti Tank
HESH	High Explosive Squash Head
HVM	Hyper Velocity Missile
Hy	Heavy
IFF	Identification Friend or Foe
II	Image Intensifier
IGB	Inner German Border
illum	illuminating
IO	Intelligence Officer
INTSUM	Intelligence Summary
IRG	Immediate Replenishment Group
IS	Internal Security
ISD	In Service Date
IT	Italy (Italian)
IW	Individual Weapon
JFHQ	Joint Force Headquarters
JHQ	Joint Headquarters
JSSU	Joint Services Signals Unit
LAD	Light Aid Detachment (REME)
L of C	Lines of Communication
LLAD	Low Level Air Defence
LO	Liaison Officer
Loc	Locating Log Logistic
LRATGW	Long Range Anti Tank Guided Weapon
LSW	Light Support Weapon

MAOT	Mobile Air Operations Team
MBT	Main Battle Tank
maint	Maintain
mat	Material
MCMV	Mine Counter Measures Vessels
med	Medical
mech	Mechanised
MFC	Mortar Fire Controller
MNAD	Multi National Airmobile Division
NE	Netherlands
MO	Medical Officer
MP	Military Police
MOD	Ministry of Defence
mob	Mobilisation
msl	missile
NAAFI	Navy, Army and Air Force Institutes
NADGE	NATO Air Defence Ground Environment
NATO	North Atlantic Treaty Organisation
NCO	Non Commissioned Officer
nec	Necessary
NL	Netherlands
NO	Norway (Norwegian)
NOK	Next of Kin
ni	Night
NORTHAG	Northern Army Group
NTR	Nothing to Report
NBC	Nuclear and Chemical Warfare
NYK	Not Yet Known
OP	Observation Post
OC	Officer Commanding
OCU	Operational Conversion Unit (RAF)
OIC	Officer in Charge
opO	Operation Order
ORBAT	Order of Battle
pax	Passengers
POL	Petrol, Oil and Lubricants
P info	Public Information
Pl	Platoon
PO	Portugal (Portuguese)
QM	Quartermaster
RAP	Rocket Assisted Projectile/Regimental Aid Post
RTM	Ready to Move
RCZ	Rear Combat Zone rec Recovery
R & D	Research and Development
rebro	Rebroadcast
recce	Reconnaissance

Regt	Regiment
RHQ	Regimental Headquarters
RMA	Rear Maintenance Area/Royal Military Academy
rft	Reinforcement
RO	Retired Officer
RSA	Royal School of Artillery
RSME	Royal School of Mechanical Engineering
RTU	Return to Unit
SACUER	Supreme Allied Commander Europe
2IC	Second in Command
SH	Support Helicopters
SHAPE	Supreme Headquarters Allied Powers Europe
sit	Situation
SITREP	Situation Report
SIB	Special Investigation Branch
SMG	Sub Machine Gun
SLR	Self Loading Rifle
smk	Smoke
SNCO	Senior Non Commissioned Officer
SP	Spain (Spanish)
Sqn	Squadron
SP	Self Propelled/Start Point
SSM	Surface to Surface Missile
SSVC	Services Sound and Vision Corporation
STOL	Short Take Off and Landing
tac	Tactical
tk	Tank
tgt	Target
TOT	Time on Target
TCP	Traffic Control Post
tpt	Transport
tp	Troop
TCV	Troop Carrying Vehicle
TLB	Top Level Nudget
TU	Turkish (Turkey)
TUL	Truck Utility Light
TUM	Truck Utility Medium
UK	United Kingdom
UKLF	United Kingdom Land Forces
UKMF	United Kingdom Mobile Force
UNCLASS	Unclassified
UXB	Unexploded Bomb
US	United States
U/S	Unserviceable
veh	Vehicle
VOR	Vehicle off the Road

WE	War Establishment
wh	Wheeled
WIMP	Whinging Incompetent Malingering Person
WMR	War Maintenance Reserve
WO	Warrant Officer
wksp	Workshop
X	Crossing (as in roads or rivers)

This publication was produced by R&F (Defence) Publications.
Editorial Office 01743-235070

The other publications in this series are:

The Royal Air Force Pocket Guide
The Armed Forces of the United Kingdom (Available early 1996)

Further copies can be obtained from :

Pen & Sword Books Ltd
47 Church Street
Barnsley S70 2AS

Telephone: 01226-734222 Fax: 01226-734438

There are special rates for purchases of more than 10 books.